Texts in Philosophy
Volume 22

The Good, the Right & the Fair
an introduction to ethics

Texts in Philosophy Series Editors
Vincent F. Hendriks   vincent@hum.ku.dk
John Symons   jsymons@utep.edu
Dov Gabbay   dov.gabbay@kcl.ac.uk

The Good, the Right & the Fair
an introduction to ethics

Mickey Gjerris,
Morten Ebbe Juul Nielsen,
and
Peter Sandøe

ISBN 978-1-84890-102-5

College Publications
Scientific Director: Dov Gabbay
Managing Director: Jane Spurr

http://www.collegepublications.co.uk

Original cover design by Laraine Welch
Cover artwork by Jacqueline Wegmann

Printed by Lightning Source, Milton Keynes, UK

Contents

Preface

The authors of this book have, for many years taught introductory philosophy courses, including an ethics module, for students in food science, natural resource management, biotechnology and other fields of applied science. We have in the past worked without a proper ethics textbook, designed specifically for such a setting. Students on such courses, in our experience, are keen to understand the ethical underpinnings of current debates regarding (for example) climate change, poverty, the use of gene technology and animal welfare, whereas they are generally not interested in philosophy in its own right. This book has been written with that in mind. It is our hope that future students and teachers in various fields of applied science, as well as others who may be interested, will find the book useful – and that it will make them wiser than they would otherwise have been.

When we embarked on writing this book, two of us worked in parallel on creating a free internet-based learning tool, the Ethics Dilemma Tool, which is available on www.ethicsinpractice.net. The e-learning tool may be used in tandem with this book, and we recommend that our readers use the tool as part of their learning process.

We are grateful for the critique and suggestions we have received from many people who have helped us along the way. Firstly, thanks are due to all the students on whom we have, over the years, tried out the ideas presented here. Secondly we owe thanks to a number of colleagues who have read and commented on the manuscript as a whole or parts of it: Anders Dahl, Trine Dich, Tina Hansen, Vagn Olsen and Clare Palmer. We also owe thanks to Paul Robinson who helped us not only by correcting our English, but also by improving the style and readability of the text in numerous ways; and to Geir Tveit who carried out the final editing of the text. We are also grateful to Professor Vincent Hendricks who helped us establish contact with College Publications. Finally we want to thank the Department of Food and Resource Economics, University of Copenhagen, and the department head, Henrik Zobbe, for generous support economically and otherwise.

Copenhagen, September 2013

Mickey Gjerris, Morten Ebbe Juul Nielsen and Peter Sandøe

1

Introduction: Thinking about ethics

In this brief introductory chapter we aim to introduce the reader to ethical thinking. The starting point for this is the fact that discussions about what is morally good and bad, right and wrong, and fair and unfair often lead to controversies and disagreements. However, as we will try to show in this chapter, ethical thinking enables people not only to become clear about their own position, but also to better appreciate others' points of view. In this way, it may help to promote understanding and tolerance, despite disagreement.

Stem cells – a promising technology, but also a cause of ethical controversy

As we all know, ethical discussion can very easily develop into heated argument. Often discussion in the area of ethics and morality (we do not here distinguish between the two) ends in disagreement, and sometimes it causes anger because the two parties cannot find any common ground. An example of this is the debate around the use of human foetuses to produce stem cells.

In 1998 James Thompson, a cell biologist at the University of Wisconsin-Madison in the USA, and his team of researchers succeeded in isolating cells from the inner cell mass of early embryos and developed the first human embryonic stem cell lines. This was the culmination of more than a hundred years of research into the therapeutic potential of human cells. It marked the beginning of the intense interest in stem cell research that has attracted huge investment since the late 1990s.

This biotechnology has huge potential. In particular, stem cells are seen as possible "spare parts" for repairing damaged or malfunctioning parts of the human body (and the technology may ultimately be used on non-human animals as well). Stem cells are undifferentiated, or "totipotent", cells. They are capable of developing into any specialized kind of body cell. The technology can potentially be used to turn some of a patient's cells – e.g. skin cells – into stem cells, which can then be used to create medically needed cells of another kind entirely. Thus if a person were suffering from a disease causing cells to be lost, or to degenerate, stem cells could, theoretically, be utilized to create new cells to replace the old ones.

The process of replacing diseased or damaged tissue has of course been used for many years; this is what is happening when patients receive transplants. However, so far it has been very difficult getting the immune system to accept the foreign tissue, and the recipients of transplants have generally had to be treated with immunosuppressive drugs for the rest of their lives. This problem could be solved if the replacement tissue was created from stem cells generated from the patient's own cells. The full potential of stem cells has not been realized, and there are significant unresolved technical problems, both in changing a patient's cells into stem cells and in turning stem cells into specific kinds of tissue. However, some researchers believe that these problems can be overcome with further research in the field.

Stem cell research relies heavily on cell lines obtained from human embryos. This is not merely a technical limitation: as you can probably guess, it is also the cause of real ethical disagreement. Therefore stem cell research has for many years been accompanied by public controversy. To some, destroying the early foetus is killing an innocent human being. For these people the use of early embryos for research involves sacrificing a human life for the common good – something they deem wholly unacceptable and immoral.

Others point out that the early human embryo is not yet recognizable, morphologically, as a human being, and has no central nervous system. They view the embryo, not as a young human being, and certainly not as a person, but as a biological resource that may be freely utilized for the benefit of developed humans. Between these two radical views lie several moderate positions. To varying degrees, these acknowledge that the early embryo may develop into a human being, but also insist that the potential of stem cell research for mankind may justify the use of human embryos for research.

One key ethical issue in the stem cell debate has been whether it is justifiable to do something that is seen by some as being morally wrong (destroying an embryo) in order to obtain something else that almost everyone considers good (finding new ways to treat serious diseases). Issues raised by the relation between the means and ends of a proposed action are not confined to the debate over stem cells. They cut across discussions of many different issues. The question whether a good end justifies what many see as morally problematic means is at the heart of many ethical debates and seems to give rise to divisions very similar to the one found here. Think about the debate about whether warfare with civilian casualties can ever be justified.

Ethical debates about new technologies

There is a tendency for technological developments that are originally met with scepticism and caution to become socially acceptable after a few years. In the 1970s, "test-tube babies" conceived in a petri dish aroused a great deal of ethical controversy. Today, one would be hard pressed to find anyone who objects to this technology in principle, although many experts have concerns about problems with which it may be associated, such as inheritable infertility.

There is no single explanation why the majority of people develop a more accepting attitude to a new technology with the passing of time. Part of the explanation may be mere habituation. We simply get used to a certain technique and the advantages it offers us. People with an optimistic view of technological progress sometimes assert, or imply, that attitudinal change occurs because our values change over time. Having experienced the technology, and having found that most of the initial objections to it were unfounded, society as a whole may become more accepting or tolerant. Technological development is therefore an important driver in the development of a society's ethical views. Indeed, according to some this is a natural and positive development.

Others claim that the reason new technologies become accepted after a while is that we become desensitized to the controversial issues by exposure to the technology over time. It is only by opposing new wrongs from the beginning that we can we halt the process of desensitization and prevent new wrongs from becoming things that we are used to doing.

Of course, there are huge geographical and cultural (not to mention historical) differences in judgements of ethical and social acceptability. For example, there seems to be a much more positive attitude to stem cell research in Protestant European countries than there is in neighbouring states with Catholic populations. **This seems to be so because in Europe – unlike in the USA – Catholic voices in favor of the sacredness of life from conception are much stronger than Protestant ones.**

So far the ethical debate about using foetal stem cells does not seem to have created any kind of public consensus, but that does not mean that those who listen may not be influenced by the arguments for and against the technology. And a key aim of this chapter – and indeed for the book as a whole – is to explore the potential for the influence of ethical arguments. Whatever the outcome of the debate on stem cell research, it remains an excellent example of the continuing discussion within society about the ethical status of human existence. "How developed should human life be to deserve protection, and can it ever be ethically justifiable to destroy human life in its early forms?" This question lies at the heart of the issue of stem cell research and the wider issue of abortion.

Is everything a matter of taste?

Debate about the moral status of early human life has being going on for decades, regrettably without bringing those involved any closer to a consensus. This means that society, and individuals working in relevant fields like biomedicine, must make ethically charged decisions in a climate of conflict and disagreement. Despite this, it may be possible for people to co-exist with a degree of mutual understanding. Ethical debates do not serve only to dig ditches. They can also serve as opportunities to understand the opinions of others, and the values and principles underlying both those opinions and one's own. This will not necessarily lead to agreement, but may lead to a more respectful attitude to the values and principles cherished by others, and to a deeper, more considered understanding of one's own values and principles.

The impossibility of finding an objective, neutral platform outside our murky world of personal values and principles has, however, led some to conclude that ethics can never leave the subjective sphere. Such a position is known as *relativism*. Relativism is the flip-side of what may be called *fundamentalism*.

Fundamentalism is the stance taken by those who think that they *just know* what is morally right and wrong without seeing the need for any kind of reflection and discussion. When people with this belief come up against conflicting views their gut reaction is not to ask for reasons but to condemn the other view as false and/or immoral. The fundamentalist stance is often linked with a religious outlook – reasonably so, since theistic moral codes are often set out in an authoritative text, such as the Bible or the Koran. However, the association is quite loose: religious belief can lead to genuine tolerance, and intolerance can be found among secular humanists.

If fundamentalism is a belief in inflexible ethical values and indisputable principles that are taken to be valid whatever other persons believe, relativism is the belief that moral claims are valid relative to individual sentiments or to culture. In the end, whether one adopts, or applies, a particular value cannot be the subject of rational discussion (in the broadest sense), because values and moral principles are subjectively made judgments that ultimately cannot be rationally supported in a way that obliges someone else to share them.

It is sometimes said that relativism is supported by the fact that throughout human history, and across different human cultures, a plurality of contrasting and even mutually exclusive values and principles has evolved. This gives way to a variety of relativism that is called cultural relativism from which it follows that just because contemporary western culture adopts, and indeed promotes, certain values – e.g. protecting the rights of the individual – it does not follow that cultures in which this is not the case are morally defective.

Initially, relativism either at the level of the individual, the social group, or the culture seems like a good solution to moral disagreement – one with the potential to prevent endless ethical debate. It acknowledges that there is a reason why we cannot come to a conclusion, and it enables us to move on. But, when it is taken to its logical conclusion, it also entails consequences that few of us are willing to accept. Most of us believe there are limits to moral tolerance: for instance, purposeless violence is surely ethically objectionable regardless of the culture or social group in which it occurs.

Again, taking the relativist stance, one cannot oppose e.g., an individual's racism on ethical grounds. In one sense there is nothing to talk about, as there is no way in which to justify an ethical viewpoint and thereby obligate others to adhere to it. You might say that relativists, in their scepticism about the reasons we can provide for our ethical values and principles, almost become fundamentalists themselves. Both parties take the view that values lie outside the sphere of rational appraisal. It is just that fundamentalists apply this view to just one set of values (their own), while relativists apply it to the various value sets adopted by different individuals and the groups to which they belong.

In practice, relativism seems to work best when the gap between the values we differ over is not too great. After all, the claim that there is no room for ethical discussion – that we should, as the saying has it, live and let live – is often greeted with acceptance, if not relief. However, few of us would be willing to accept that it is ethically unproblematic to suppress a black woman because of the colour of her skin, and because of her sex, just because the suppression takes place within a framework of different ethical values.

Ethical pluralism: the middle ground?

It is socially prudent to be tolerant of the values of others, yet relativism implies that one does not need to defend one's own values, or devote time to understanding the values of others. However, it seems that, although we cannot always find common ground from which to pass ethical judgements, we do make evaluations using standards that exclude at least some ethical values and principles. Somewhere, between fundamentalism and relativism, there is space in which to reflect on values and ideals and, to some degree at least, pass judgment on them.

This is what we appear to do, anyway. Most of us, in practice, accept a position that can be labelled *ethical pluralism*. This position, on the one hand, accepts that mutually exclusive values can exist at the same time without there being a definitive way of deciding which one is better. On the other hand, the ethical pluralist maintains that there are limits to what can be claimed as ethical, although admittedly these limits are rather broad.

Pluralism seems partly to be based on the value of *tolerance*. The idea is that, within certain limits, people should be allowed to make up their own minds on questions of right and wrong, but that they can and should live peacefully together despite their moral differences. Thus one person may reach the conclusion that it is morally wrong to rear and kill animals for food and therefore becomes a vegetarian or vegan, while another person thinks it is acceptable to eat animal products as long as these come from animals that have lived a decent life. These two people may be good friends. They may dine together, respecting each other's choice of food and moral stance towards animals.

However it should be noted that the value of tolerance may itself limit how much disagreement can be accommodated within the pluralist stance. This is because, in its nature, tolerance excludes intolerance. So, for example, a pluralist will not be inclined to accept racist or sexist views, precisely because they are intolerant toward specific groups of people for no good moral reason. Pluralism leaves room where, through careful reflection, each of us can try to make up her or his own mind in a qualified, or considered, way and find some common ground from where we can at least get some consensus on which values and actions are ethically acceptable. In light of this view moral thinking helps us when we have to choose between different values and principles in a situation in which we are unsure of the right choice, and it allows us to think about and discuss the moral views of others.

However, to be able to think about and discuss values it is necessary to put those values into words, and, in a way, this is what this book is about.

Putting ethical values into words: ethical theories

In the course of more than two thousand years of philosophical reflection on ethics in the West (there are also other cultural traditions which will not be covered here) a number of theories of the good, the right and the fair have developed. The present book is an attempt to present and explain these theories to those with little or no background in philosophy.

Theories are useful in that they impose structure on our thoughts about what is good and bad, right and wrong, and fair and unfair. However, they can also be rather abstract and dry. To bring things down to earth, therefore, we have tried throughout the book to use vivid, realistic examples when explaining the theories.

We speak of *theories* in the plural here; and this is a deliberate choice. There is wide agreement about the importance of ethics, but there is, as we have already indicated, much less agreement about the kinds of considerations – the theoretical assumptions, if you like – that underpin ethical judgements and beliefs.

To us, the variety of theories and arguments in ethics is intellectually stimulating, and worth considering and studying – more stimulating, indeed, than just sticking to one theory. And we do not *advocate* any specific moral theory in this book. Nor do we provide the reader with determinate *answers* to specific moral questions, representing these as *the* correct answers. Rather, we set out important considerations that can be, and have been, advanced for and against particular opinions. Our aim is to stimulate readers to make up their own minds.

On the other hand, we cannot claim to be entirely neutral or impartial. Each author has his own sympathies (not necessarily the same as those of the others), and almost certainly we have not succeeded in fully concealing them. Also we cannot claim to present *all* the relevant positions and theories in any particular case. What we have done is to focus on the arguments and theories that we take to be *central* either in the philosophical literature or in our own understanding of normative ethics and its applications.

What can be gained by discussing ethical values and principles?

As mentioned, ethical discussions in the public domain today often seem to result in the further entrenchment of values and the widening of the gap between opposing viewpoints. We believe that this can be explained, to a large extent, by the underlying aim of many ethical debates: to produce a consensus, or at least a compromise. Against this, we would suggest that the purpose of discussing ethics is not, first and foremost, to reach decisions that all can agree to without reservation, but rather to gain knowledge of the ethical perspectives involved in the debate.

Ethical discussions represent an opportunity to understand the values of others, both from the historical and the normative perspective. The historical perspective means listening to the ethical values of others, and to the stories through which those values developed. The normative perspective means trying to understand the reasons why other people's values are not always the same as our own. One should both have to try to understand the other and help the other understand oneself.

This approach, as we have said, does not necessarily lead to agreement. But it will make us a bit wiser about why we disagree in that we will gain a deeper understanding of the ethical perspective of other human beings, as well as our own. Viewed in this light, ethical discussion, instead of acting like a wedge driving two parties further apart, as happens all too often, instead may act as a flashlight that illuminates the discussion.

Finally, we claim, along with the German philosopher Jürgen Habermas, who developed what is called *discourse ethics*, that being able to justify one's actions in the light of certain values and principles is also a way of showing respect to other human beings. It means that we take them seriously enough to feel an obligation to explain – to *justify* – our views and actions.

Decision time

If it is true that ethical discussion is to encourage us to respect the views of others, it is also true that this respect can be used in the decision-making process. At some point a decision generally has to be taken. We can discuss the ethical issues related to stem cell research for a long time, but at some point we need to make societal decisions about whether or not to proceed with the research. At this point, the knowledge gained in ethical debate can be used to inform our actions in a way reflecting the values of those who disagree with us.

Often we have to do one thing or another. We have just two options: we proceed with foetal stem cell research, or we do not. However, we can take the fact that some people find this kind of research ethically problematic into consideration, and do our utmost to search for alternatives, while progressing with the research in as careful a manner as possible. This will not satisfy everyone, but it is a way of creating a socially robust solution to our ethical disagreements – a solution that alienates as few people as possible.

It is one thing to live in a society in which one's values are not shared by the majority of citizens. Such a situation is impossible to avoid in a democratic society. But it is quite another to live in a society in which one's values are not even heard, and in which no attempt is made to understand them by those who eventually take the decisions. It is surely not unreasonable to suppose that the first kind of society might well involve peaceful co-existence, while the second is less likely to be like this.

It is of course true that not all moral disagreements can be peacefully settled in this way. In the last chapters of the book we shall consider how far we can get with the pluralist approach we have recommended and identify what could be done when it is not enough.

Key points

- This chapter discussed the role of ethical thinking in dealing with practical questions. We recognized at the outset that some moral debates do not have a conclusion to which all can agree. For example, in the debate over the moral status of human foetuses some people claim that it is morally wrong to use, and eventually kill, human foetuses, while others see this as acceptable when it serves an important purpose – say, in biomedical research.

- Two positions, both of which claim that ethical thinking and discussion have a very limited role, were presented. One is ethical *fundamentalism*, according to which one just knows what is morally right and wrong without any need for reflection or discussion. The other is ethical *relativism*, which claims that moral values and principles are relative to different social groups and cultures, and therefore cannot be discussed or assessed.

- Both positions were criticized. A middle position was sketched, called *ethical pluralism,* according to which there are limits to what can be claimed to be ethically right, although these limits are rather broad. Pluralism is underpinned by the value of tolerance, and it turned out that this is a value that also places limits on what can be considered an acceptable ethical stance.

- The notion of an *ethical theory* was then introduced. An ethical theory is an attempt to explain an ethical stance by trying to work it out systematically and think about its more general implications in practice. In this book several competing ethical theories will be set out, so that the reader can think through a number of ethical stances.

- We suggested that, by working through different ethical theories, readers will not only be encouraged to make up their own minds in an informed way, but also be better placed to understand and appreciate the views of people who take a different one.

- As a society we often *have* to take decisions on controversial ethical issues – e.g. whether or not to allow biomedical research involving human foetuses. These decisions are very unlikely to satisfy everyone, but if we all give due consideration to views that we disagree with, we may be able to reach wider acceptance of the decisions that are made on controversial ethical issues.

Part I

The Good

2
Welfare

What is the ultimate end, or goal, of human life? In making the decisions we make, and acting in the way we do, what are we seeking to achieve? The immediate goals of our endeavours are extremely diverse and often rather obvious: to finish a book, to win a game of tennis, to avoid the rain. The question above is not about these, however. It is about the overarching purpose of what we do. Are the diverse and obvious goals of daily life united by a single, less obvious goal? In one sense, this question has a fairly straightforward answer. We are all familiar with the idea that life can go more or less well. At any point in time, different people will have different levels of well-being. Picking up this idea, philosophers often talk about an individual's welfare, and it is a short step from this to the idea that welfare is the elusive, overarching goal of human existence: it is what makes life worth living, and other goals are ultimately only worth pursuing if they serve to promote it. This raises a new question, however. What exactly is welfare? What does it consist of – what makes life go well? Can well-being really be boiled down to a single ingredient? Some philosophers have defended positive answers to these questions. Many of them have also concluded that ethical questions are, in the end, questions about welfare and nothing else. Is this right? Is morality all about the promotion of welfare?

You ask a friend how things are going. He says "Good, thanks. I managed to get time to finish the Stephen King novel I've been reading. Later, at tennis, I finally beat a guy ranked higher than me, and actually the match was over so quickly I was home before it started raining tonight". You are a little envious, but you don't show it. "Sounds great", you say.

We understand conversations like this without difficulty. Clearly, things have gone well for your friend. Equally clearly, his day would have gone less well had he been interrupted while trying to read, or lost at tennis, or got soaked on the way home. Moral philosophers, and economists interested in questions about the quality of life, would say that your friend's level of *well-being*, or *welfare*, has remained high through the day.

Since the ancient Greeks, personal well-being has attracted serious academic interest. This is for a number of reasons. To begin with, personal well-being has fascinated thinkers in its own right simply because it isn't immediately obvious what it is. What exactly does the fact that your day, or your life, is "going well" involve? Do the various specific activities and experiences that make life go well have a single feature in common which explains why they raise your level of welfare? For example, do tennis and reading increase your welfare because they make you feel happy? Really? Didn't the creepy Stephen King story actually make you feel ill at ease? Or is it impossible to boil the idea of well-being down to just one ingredient – all we can say is that a variety of activities, achievements and experiences constitute it? Thus the tennis victory made you happy, but getting home before the rain simply meant that you didn't have the unpleasant sensation of being cold and wet. Happiness and the avoidance of unpleasant sensations may have quite a lot to do with one another, but they are not the same thing.

These questions about the *nature* of welfare are the basic ones. They are basic, not in the sense of being easy, like basic arithmetic, but in the sense that they are fundamental: they need to be answered first, because other questions about welfare cannot be addressed properly unless we know what welfare is.

Without doubt, the biggest "other question" here is about the relation between welfare and morality, or (as we shall generally say) *ethics*. It is easy to see that ethical principles must have something to do with well-being. Moral obligations and prohibitions often seem to be asserted on the basis that unethical conduct causes suffering. The fact that one person's behaviour damages another's well-being automatically leads us to ask whether the behaviour is acceptable – by which we mean ethically acceptable. Often, of course, we conclude that it is not. Consider, for example, the following passages from a paper published in the scientific journal *Nature*:

> *The World Health Organisation estimates that the warming and precipitation trends due to anthropogenic climate change of the past 30 years already claim over 150,000 lives annually. Many prevalent human diseases are linked to climate fluctuations, from cardiovascular mortality and respiratory illnesses due to heatwaves, to altered transmission of infectious diseases and malnutrition from crop failures ...*

The regions with the greatest burden of climate-sensitive diseases are also the regions with the lowest capacity to adapt to the new risks. Africa – the continent where an estimated 90% of malaria occurs – has some of the lowest per capita emissions of the greenhouse gases that cause global warming. In this sense, global climate change not only presents new region-specific health risks, but also a global ethical challenge. (Patz et al. 2005, our emphasis)

The train of thought in the second excerpt is so familiar we hardly notice the transitions. The people suffering most from climate change are those least able to deal with the problems and least responsible for causing them in the first place. Isn't it entirely obvious that the fact that these persons are suffering, or will suffer introduces a global *ethical* challenge?

Positive and negative welfare

Very few people would question the idea that ethical principles have something to do with well-being. In illustrating this idea we have focused on a case where ethically questionable behaviour causes suffering – in other words, reduced or *negative* welfare. But is ethics only about this? As soon as we introduce the notion of negative welfare it becomes apparent that there must also be *positive* welfare. In the example at the beginning of this chapter your friend didn't just avoid suffering. He also enjoyed positive states. He felt satisfaction at finishing the book and a sense of achievement on winning at tennis.

This raises a new question. Is ethics solely about limiting conduct with a negative impact on welfare, or do we also have an ethical obligation to actively promote, or maximize, the welfare of those we can assist?

The idea that we are required to promote the welfare of other people – that it would be unethical not to do so – is likely to be controversial. Most people would readily agree that it is morally objectionable if others suffer as the result of my actions. But it is less obvious that I am obliged to ensure others don't miss out on something that would increase their levels of welfare, such as an opportunity to watch a gripping drama on television.

One of the great philosophers of the twentieth-century, Karl Popper (1902–1994), argued that we are not required to promote the well-being of others. Our sole aim should instead be to reduce avoidable suffering for everybody as much as possible. In *The Open Society and Its Enemies*, first published in 1945, Popper suggests that: "it adds to the clarity of ethics if we formulate our demands negatively, i.e. if we demand the elimination of suffering rather than the promotion of happiness" (Popper 1966, p. 285).

This is certainly a tempting idea, but it was soon pointed out that it has a nasty implication: If your sole aim is to eliminate suffering, it will be hard to avoid the conclusion that you have the obligation to take the lives of everyone (including yourself!) painlessly if you can, because in this way you can eliminate all suffering once and for all:

> *Suppose that a ruler controls a weapon capable of instantly and painlessly destroying the human race. Now it is empirically certain that there would be some suffering before all those alive on any proposed destruction day were to die in the natural course of events. Consequently the use of the weapon is bound to diminish suffering, and would be the ruler's duty ...* (Smart 1958, p. 542)

The point here is not only that the mass killing would lead to an end to all suffering, but also that any alternative course of action will lead to at least some suffering. Any person is bound to experience negative welfare at some point, since even in the best of lives there are bound to be periods of disease, grief and the like. So no cause of action could be as efficient as mass killing in preventing suffering.

The idea that there is an ethical requirement to kill the entire human race is patently absurd. Critics of Popper therefore interpret this speculation as a reason that we cannot be obliged only to eliminate suffering – that ethics is about promoting positive welfare as well as limiting its negative counterpart.

Psychological hedonism

Let us now try to get a bit clearer about what welfare is. One view we need to understand here is *hedonism*. Hedonism, when philosophers discuss it, is not an enthusiastic attitude to orgies, food and alcohol. It is the less exciting view that welfare consists of the presence of enjoyable mental states, such as pleasure, and the absence of painful, or unpleasant, ones. The theory is realistic, in one sense of the word: It allows that unpleasant states will figure, unavoidably, in the lives of anyone, including those who enjoy themselves most of the time and thus have a reasonably high level of welfare. The hedonist position is simply that your life goes better the more your enjoyable mental states outweigh the unpleasant ones.

Hedonism can be either psychological or normative in nature. The psychological theory says that human beings *are* in fact always motivated to act by their anticipation of pleasure and pain. The normative theory says that, ultimately, pleasure and the avoidance of pain are the only things *worth* striving for: the central idea is that pleasure is the only thing that makes life go well, the sole ultimate ingredient of well-being.

There is something immediately implausible about psychological hedonism. It is certainly true that in our conduct we are guided by expectations of pleasure and a desire to avoid pain. However, we also seem to do things for other reasons: we often want to complete the tasks we have started (e.g. tidying the garden at dusk), to discover important truths (e.g. about illnesses), to be friendly or decent (e.g. by texting a newcomer to the class). On grey Monday mornings the most pleasurable thing to do might be to stay in bed, but most of us are still motivated to get up and get on with things.

If it is to be at all credible, then, psychological hedonism must account for the fact that many of our immediate motivations have little to do with the attainment of pleasure. The obvious adjustment here is to claim that we are motivated by expectations of "over-all" pleasure, or our net pleasure, measured over the long term. This adjustment allows the psychological hedonist to accommodate apparent counterexamples such as those mentioned above. The hedonist can say that people who appear to be acting in ways that do not promote their own pleasure are acting strategically. They are focusing, probably wisely, on the longer term – on how to maximize their positive mental states throughout life. This focus makes perfect sense from within the hedonist perspective.

The idea that personal pleasure is the motivation underlying everything people do may seem provocative, and even mean-spirited. On the other hand, it is very much in line with the more reductionist views of man's nature inspired by thinkers such as Charles Darwin (1809–1882) and Sigmund Freud (1856–1939). Whether one likes the idea or not, it does have philosophical supporters today. It remains a serious, if controversial, hypothesis.

Normative hedonism

In contrast with its psychological counterpart, the normative version of hedonism is not vulnerable to the objection that, as a matter of fact, we pursue things other than pleasure. It claims, not that we actually are motivated solely by pleasure in life, but rather that we *ought* to be motivated this way. The classic formulation of this normative position was presented by the English lawyer and philosopher Jeremy Bentham (1748–1832). Bentham was a social reformer who thought that under the influence of religion and tradition, many institutions promoted ideals and behaviour that were detrimental to human happiness.

Against the prevailing norms of his time, Bentham argued in a famous passage that the only measure there can be of the value, or worth, of an activity is the amount of pleasure it gives to those involved in it:

> *The utility of all these arts and sciences ... the value which they possess, is exactly in proportion to the pleasure they yield ... Prejudice apart, the game of push-pin [a game played by children] is of equal value with the arts and sciences of music and poetry. If the game of push-pin furnish more pleasure, it is more valuable than either.* (Bentham 1830, p. 206)

Elsewhere Bentham acknowledges that for some people poetry and music may be more gratifying, or pleasurable, than playing simple games. He insists, however, that this merely tells us something about the people in question, and their capacity for pleasure, not that poetry and music have greater value. The value, or worth, of every activity should be judged solely by the quantity of pleasure it gives.

Notice that the normative hedonist need not hold that the only thing you could possibly have *reason* to do is pursue your own pleasure. The position is simply that pleasure alone has value – pleasure alone enhances welfare. Historically, this position has very often been combined with the view that, morally speaking, we should always act in such a way as to maximize the quantity of pleasure there is in the world. It is easy to see that sometimes a moral demand of this sort will clash with self-interested pursuit of pleasure. An individual with a strong sense of duty might have good reason to undertake training in mathematics and other difficult subjects in order to become a doctor, even though the training gives them little pleasure!

Here we are witnessing a gap opening up between questions about the nature of welfare (does it consist solely in pleasant mental states?) and questions about what we are ethically required to do (should we always act so as to maximize everyone's pleasant mental states?) These are separate questions. The normative hedonist, in giving a pleasure-based answer to the first, is not forced to embrace some crude form of ethical egoism. He can reject the outlandish idea that selfish pursuit of one's own pleasure is ethical. In short: what is *good* for a person is a distinct question from what it is *right* for the person to do.

It is important to realize that hedonism and the idea that we should maximize well-being have had a profound effect on the morality of modern, liberal societies. Bentham himself, with his background as a lawyer, was keen to reform the penal system. When a crime is committed, the victims of the crime normally suffer. However, punishment itself often just adds more suffering, although now the perpetrator suffers. According to Bentham, punishment can be justified only if it has good consequences such as preventing the perpetrator from committing further crimes, or deterring others from committing similar crimes. However, much of the punishment Bentham saw could not plausibly be justified in this way. Bentham was instrumental in promoting the kind of thinking about punishment that focuses on rehabilitation and prevention rather than retribution. Today, this kind of thinking about punishment is highly influential in most western countries, although of course some people continue to take a "retributivist" view.

But are pleasure and the absence of pain really the only things that count when it comes to the question: "How well is your life going?" Not all agree on this.

Is it better to be a sad Socrates than a happy pig?

Bentham, like other advocates of normative hedonism, believed that a person's well-being is determined by their *net* pleasure. The "net" here is important. The key thing is how much pleasure you have relative to (or minus) the pain and other negative mental states you experience. So, while it makes sense to avoid pain and other forms of negative welfare as far as possible, it can be rational to accept a certain amount of negative welfare if this is a means of avoiding larger amounts of negative welfare, or of gaining a larger amount of positive welfare.

For example, physical exercise may be quite unpleasant in the short term. However, exercise may prevent one from suffering from poor health later in life, and some even claim that after one has endured a period of habituation, exercise can actually be quite pleasant. So the net effect of a running regime may be positive.

According to Bentham the only thing that matters is the *quantity* of pleasure. Quantity is measured by the intensity and duration of a pleasure. This is why Bentham says in the passage quoted above "the game of push-pin is of equal value with the arts and sciences of music and poetry. If the game of push-pin furnish more pleasure, it is more valuable than either". Bentham would allow, of course, that sometimes the long-term gains of more demanding activities such as mastering a musical instrument are greater than the short-term costs (the boredom of playing scales over and over again). Over sufficient time, a person's welfare may well be better served by work than play.

Even with this qualification, many subsequent writers have found the idea that all pleasures are equal in value implausible, and even offensive. John Stuart Mill (1806–1873), who was a student of Bentham's, and his follower in many respects, famously denied that all pleasures contribute to well-being to the same degree. In a famous passage, Mill says that

> ... it is better to be a human being dissatisfied than a pig satisfied; better to be Socrates dissatisfied than a fool satisfied. And if the fool, or the pig, are of a different opinion, it is because they only know their own side of the question. (Mill 1863, p. 9)

What Mill seems to have in mind here is that we make *qualitative* distinctions between different kinds of pleasure – or, as he puts it, satisfaction. Bentham accords the same value to the pleasures of poetry and playing children's games. Mill seems to claim that some kinds of pleasure are simply more valuable than others: two pleasures may have exactly the same intensity and duration, yet differ in value, so that one makes a greater contribution to well-being. Mill had a view – by today's standards a rather conventional, Victorian view – on which kinds of pleasure are the most valuable. For him, the pleasure derived from poetry appreciation has greater value than that associated with the enjoyment of food, for example.

Mill marked this view by speaking of "higher pleasures" and "lower pleasures". Of course, modern admirers of Mill need not follow him in claiming that it is better to read poetry than it is to dine well. We are less stuffy these days. Nevertheless, there may be something in Mill's division of the pleasures. Conceivably, a devoted, life-long collector of matchboxes and a successful international theatre director could have lives involving equal quantities of pleasure, but would we be prepared to say that their lives were equally rewarding? Many of us would hesitate to do so. We would feel instinctively that the director got the better deal.

Mill's twenty-first century advocates can also agree that some needs have to be fulfilled before one starts engaging in higher pleasures. Were Mill alive today, he might for example, accept the popular hierarchy of needs developed by the American psychologist Abraham Maslow (1908–1970), according to which a number of basic needs must be fulfilled before an individual will get anything out of attempting to realize the higher pleasures connected with human creativity.

The main point of Mill's *qualitative hedonism* is that a pleasure is not a simple index of well-being. Some pleasures are more valuable intrinsically – that is, in their own right, and not just because of their consequences – than others. What matters, from a self-interested point of view, is not only to obtain the greatest possible amount of pleasure (net, after deducting pain), but rather to get the right kind of pleasures, including those connected with aesthetic and intellectual activities. In some cases it may be worth sacrificing some lower pleasures to gain access to higher ones. In short, it may be better to be Socrates dissatisfied than a pig satisfied.

Mill's view is likely to be in keeping with the priorities of many of his readers (if you don't enjoy higher pleasures, you probably won't read a philosophy book). However, one may ask whether, in discarding Bentham's relatively simple theory, Mill is really sticking with hedonism. Bentham's position is clearly that pleasure, and pleasure alone, is valuable. Is Mill able to say that? He seems rather to be saying that pleasure, or satisfaction, is the basic ingredient in well-being, but not the sole ingredient. It matters *what kind of* pleasure it is, but still pleasure is a necessary condition for something being valuable. Some moral philosophers have moved away from Mill here. Siding with Mill, against Bentham, they accept that poetry is "better" than push-pin, but against Mill they prefer to say that some activities and achievements are valuable *in their own right,* quite apart from how much pleasure they are associated with. Some writers have devised lists of the kinds of thing (knowledge, friendship, and so on) that give a person well-being, and as a consequence this view is now known as the "objective list theory". The objective list theory represents a straightforward rejection of the idea that pleasure is the only positive contributor to personal well-being.

Mill would probably insist that even if his theory asserts that different kinds of activity contribute in different ways to a good life, they all have one thing in common: the positive activities involve an experience of various forms of pleasant mental states, and the negative ones involve unpleasant mental states. On this basis, Mill might well plead that he is still a hedonist, in the sense that welfare is about mental states and experiences.

So, now is a good time to look at a famous argument for the anti-hedonist view that well-being is not constructed exclusively out of mental states, i.e. is not just a matter of what you experience.

The experience machine

Hedonists hold that, fundamentally, the level of your well-being is determined solely by your mental states. Very roughly, if you *feel* well you *are* well – and this remains true even if your felt happiness or contentment is based wholly on a mistaken belief about the situation you are actually in. However, it can be argued that welfare is about what happens in the world as well as what happens in our minds. The American philosopher Robert Nozick (1938–2002) once presented a powerful argument of this sort involving the following thought-experiment.

Suppose there was an experience machine that would give you any experience you desired. Superduper neuropsychologists could stimulate your brain so that you would think and feel you were writing a great novel, or making a friend, or reading an interesting book. All the time you would be floating in a tank, with electrodes attached to your brain. Should you plug into this machine for life, preprogramming your life's desires? ... Of course, while in the tank you won't know that you're there; you'll think it's all actually happening. Others can also plug in to have the experiences they want, so there's no need to stay unplugged to serve them. (Ignore problems such as who will service the machines if everyone plugs in.) Would you plug in? What else can matter to us, other than how our lives feel from the inside? (Nozick 1974, p. 43)

Very few people would answer Nozick's question with an enthusiastic "Yes, I certainly would!" Nozick therefore infers that something other than "how our lives feel from inside" matters: real friendship, real literary composition, and so on, make us better off than their simulated counterparts.

How should the committed hedonist respond to this argument? First, strictly speaking the argument does not show that hedonism is false. Rather it seems to show that most of us do not *believe* in hedonism. Formally, it can be reconstructed this way: (1) if we believed in hedonism, we would gladly plug in to the experience machine; but (2) we aren't willing to plug in to the experience machine; so (3) we do not believe in hedonism. This gives the hedonist a little space in which to manoeuvre, since it is one thing to point out that many people intuitively reject a theory and quite another to assert that the theory is false. In the mid-nineteenth century many people would have intuitively rejected Darwin's theory of evolution, but this would not have demonstrated that Darwin's theory was false.

To this it might be replied that a scientific theory, such as the theory of evolution, and an ethical theory, such as hedonism, are not analogous in the way this response assumes. Scientific theories are about mind-independent reality and therefore the theory can be true or false independently of whether we think it is true or false. Ethical theories, on the other hand, are not about mind-independent reality – at least, not in the same way. Rather they attempt to rationalize and explain what is in our minds when we make ethical choices. It is therefore unclear what could be meant by the assertion that normative hedonism is true, even if no one believes it.

A second line of resistance available to the hedonist focuses on premise (1) of Nozick's argument. There are in fact a number of reasons why someone might be reluctant to plug in to the experience machine, besides having, at some level, anti-hedonist convictions. One obvious reason is a lack of trust in the rather casually given assurance that the machine will deliver the promised goods in the way claimed. Deep-seated human aversion to risk may simply be such that we are bound to be sceptical about the experience machine, and this, rather than our anti-hedonist convictions, may explain why people are reluctant to plug in.

Finally, some hedonists may question premise (2) of Nozick's argument. They may insist that, in fact, most people *would* hook up to the machine if it really were available. To back up this claim, they could point to the fact that a lot of people spend a great deal of time hooked up to reality TV, computer games, and other "experience machines".

Against this, it can be argued that the fact that many people spend time hooked up to what are virtually experience machines does not mean that they would be willing to plug in to Nozick's experience machine, and thereby leave reality forever. Doing the latter involves a much bigger step, obviously. It involves experiential *severance* from reality. So perhaps the best conclusion is that people do care about various things other than their own inner lives. For the promise of a life of highly enjoyable but false experiences, would you agree to an arrangement ensuring you never encounter your loved ones again? Or would you give up training for the Olympics for enjoyable but false gold medal experiences? It is not a very inviting prospect, is it? So the appeal of a normative, hedonist theory claiming that we ought to care only about our inner lives seems limited, to say the least.

Suppose Nozick's experience machine argument is sound. Where should we go from here? Basically, there are two possible directions in which to go when one abandons hedonism. One move, as suggested in the previous section, is to adopt an "objective list" account of what matters in life. Such an account would not prevent one from agreeing that pleasant mental states are important for a good life. One would merely insist that other factors, such as achievement and close personal relationships, matter. Of course, achievement and relationships with others typically lead to pleasant mental states, but it may be claimed that the value of the states entirely depends on the achievement and/or close personal relationships being real and not just figments of the imagination.

This path would oblige us to abandon Bentham's ambition to deliver a simple, clear-cut account of what matters. Another path, which avoids this consequence, is to move towards a *preference theory of welfare*. We turn to this theory now.

Preference theory of welfare

In essence the experience machine argument asks: What would you *prefer* to do? It turns out – if the argument is successful – that we would prefer a life lived in the real world. We prefer to have genuine access to reality, to friends, to authentic achievement, and so forth, rather than being restricted to mere experiences, however enjoyable those experiences might be. Advocates of the objective list theory conclude from this that the various specific things we prefer to engage with – such as friendship, achievement and discovery – are *themselves* constituents of welfare. They generally assume that these constituents can in principle be presented in a list, although in fact it is unclear whether any such list would command general approval. The purpose of this list is to catalogue the things that make life go well, or *perfect* a person's life – hence the alternative label for this view, "perfectionism". A good life, one which contains maximum well-being, will have most, if not all, of the items that appear on the list in it: friendships, deep knowledge, high levels of achievement, and whatever else the perfectionist view stipulates.

But a quite different conclusion can be drawn from the experience machine. The thing all the listed items have in common, as the experience machine argument itself reveals, is that they are what we *prefer* to have. But if this is so, why not say that a person's well-being is determined simply and solely by preference-satisfaction? My well-being increases when preferences of mine are satisfied. It decreases when my preferences are frustrated. This is the core idea of the preference- or desire-satisfaction theory of welfare – the *preference* or *desire theory*, for short.

According to the preference theory, the good life is defined in terms of preference-satisfaction. A good life is one in which the person in question gets what she or he wants. To see the difference between this and the objective list theory, imagine making a good friend at college. Both theories say you are better off as a result. However, the list theory says that is the *friendship* that makes you better off, while the preference theory says that it is the bare fact that you have *got what you want*, or prefer, that does this. Of course, you might want something that is perhaps not on an objective list – casual sex, for instance. Preference theory says that if you get something of this sort you are better off. The list theorist must deny that. Conversely, you might make no effort to obtain something that is on the list. You might shun achievement, for example. Would that make your life go less well? Objective list theory says that it would (assuming achievement is on the list). The preference theorist will say that it depends. If at some level you wanted to achieve, you are passing over an opportunity to enhance your well-being. If you genuinely didn't want whatever counts as achievement, you would not have added to your well-being by getting it.

The preference view has several advantages. First, it is simple, and in philosophy, as in science, a simple theory explaining a given dataset is always to be preferred over more complex theories handling the same data.

Secondly, preference theory sits well with central elements of economic theory and other social sciences in which welfare is defined in terms of "revealed" preferences. (Revealed preferences are those inferred from market behaviour, or purchasing habits. The contrast is with "declared" preferences, or what people *say* they prefer. The two often fail to coincide. Thus interviewees actually buy less organic food than they claim.)

Finally, preference theory sits well with the kind of liberal political pluralism and tolerance widely accepted, especially in western democracies, these days. The objective list account can be recruited to tell people how to live their lives – rather as the lists of the seven deadly sins and seven heavenly virtues might some centuries ago. Preference theory cannot be used in this way. Appropriating the list theorist's language, it can say: people's lives are perfected by their getting what they want, but quite what they want is up to them.

The Australian philosopher Peter Singer, one of the leading proponents of the preference theory, offers the following argument for the theory:

> ... I cannot deny that for me, a good life is one in which my own considered, informed preferences are maximally satisfied. If I hold this judgment in a form that makes no particular reference to myself – as I must, if it is to be a moral judgment as I understand the term – then I must hold that this is true for others as well, other things being equal. (Singer 2002)

Looking at his own life, Singer concludes that his well-being is best served when his preferences are satisfied as much as possible. He claims that if this conclusion is treated as a value judgement (or what he calls "a moral judgement") it must apply to others as well (we will return to a discussion of this so-called requirement of universalizability in chapters 3 and 5): for each and every person, quality of life improves as more and more of their preferences are satisfied. Quite generally, there is a clear link between well-being and *what a person wants to do*. Ultimately, no one, according to Singer, is in a position to tell another that he is wrong when he says that certain things matter in his life – although, of course, strategic advice (e.g. if you want this, shouldn't you be doing that?) has a place.

More support for preference theory comes from the fact that it is able to deal with the problem faced by hedonism that different people seem to care differently about mental states. Some people have low pain threshold. They have an aversion to relatively mild pain. Others, more stoical in outlook, have a high threshold and only care about pain experience when it is more intense. Bentham's hedonism is committed to the view that pain at some rather mild level is as bad for the stoic as it is for the more sensitive sufferer. That doesn't look plausible. On the preference theory, however, the two cases are suitably differentiated, since well-being tracks the strength of the sufferer's negative preference, rather than the pain itself.

A final point: some readers are bound to think: Aren't preferences mental states? Surely the preference theory is exposed to the experience machine argument in exactly the same way that hedonism was. A preference for spaghetti bolognese can be satisfied artificially by the experience machine, but on reflection we realize that it matters to us whether the preference is fulfilled by a real visit to a restaurant. Hence preference theory is incorrect.

This objection can be countered by the adherer of preference theory by pointing to that the preference for the preference for the bolognese is a desire for real bolognese, not just the experience of eating bolognese. Precisely because of this, it can be satisfied only if you actually eat the bolognese. If a machine were programmed to give you an artificial experience of doing so, the experience would *not* satisfy your preference, no matter how convincing it was. So in fact the preference theory supports the Nozickian insight that well-being is connected with what we actually do, not just what we seem to be doing.

Singer qualifies the link between the good life and preference-satisfaction in two very important ways. He says that the preferences that count are those which are *considered* and *informed.* With these two qualifications, he aims to handle two types of situations. The first arises when a preference is not stable because the person with it is in the grip of a mood or whim. The second occurs when the person is not adequately informed about his or her preference(s). When these qualifications are examined, problems emerge – as we shall explain in the next section.

What does it take for preferences to be considered and informed?

Suppose you have just finished watching a very engaging documentary about "extreme" camping when a friend drops by and invites you to join a three-week holiday in the wilderness, far away from any kind of emergency help. You are still pretty excited about the documentary, and you cheerfully accept the invitation. However, on the camping trip itself you realise you don't really like the simple living it requires. You hate getting up in the morning without a proper bath, and you really don't like not having a comfortable bed to sleep in. For you, the trip is basically a disaster.

In this case, the satisfaction of your original preference for an extreme camping holiday didn't add to your well-being. So it seems that for the satisfaction of a preference to make a positive contribution quality of life it must persist, and be stable, over the period during which it is satisfied. Before acting on a preference it is therefore important to consider whether it is something one really wants. Of course, this is much easier to say than to do. In practice it can be difficult to know what one's considered preferences are, and some people have to go up quite a number of blind alleys before they find out, if they ever do!

To see the point of the other qualification Singer mentions – that preferences should be informed. Take smoking. Today most people, in the western world at least, are aware that smoking reduces life expectancy because it is causally associated with lung cancer and other serious diseases. However, this was not the case 50 or 60 years ago. People who were young at that time would probably not have been told that smoking posed a danger. Quite the contrary, in fact, since, in its advertising, the tobacco industry promoted the idea that smoking was safe. The industry was also involved in other efforts to cast doubt on the growing scientific evidence that smoking is dangerous.

Most of the elderly people who once smoked and now suffer from tobacco-related diseases now probably strongly regret having started to smoke when they were young. At the time they had a clear enough preference for cigarettes. However, given the lack of publicly available information at that time, and given the efforts of the tobacco industry to distort the research that was emerging, their preference was uninformed. So it is not just any preference whose satisfaction contributes to well-being: the preferences that raise a person's level of welfare need to be based on reasonably full and accurate information (especially about consequences).

However, even where information is readily available people may ignore it. Far fewer people in the western world smoke today than in the past, but still many people smoke, and many young people take up the habit. Must the preference theorist say that smoking makes a positive contribution to the quality of these people's lives?

A positive answer to this question makes the preference theory look rather implausible. Perhaps the advocate of preference theory should instead say something like this: in many or all cases smoking does not contribute to a person's quality of life, because people very often don't really consider their preference to smoke in the light of the right information, sensibly weighted, before they start, and because later they then cannot readily stop even if they want to. The preference theory now looks more plausible from a common-sense point of view. However, it has lost its simplicity – which, as we saw above, was one of its selling points. There is no longer a simple, direct link between getting what you want and doing well. Buried in that link is a more complex set of subsidiary requirements: you must be in possession of "the right" information, "sensibly weighted", and you must be able to jettison, or at any rate stop acting on, your preference following a change of heart.

What we can see happening here is essentially this. A pleasingly clear, uncomplicated account of well-being is being replaced by more elaborate account in which elements other than preference appear. And, looking closely, one sees that explicitly normative notions, like the notion of the "the right information" and "sensible weighting" are now surfacing in the account. But expressions like these raise as many questions as the notion of well-being itself. We might well ask, then, just how much progress has been made.

So Singer's requirement that preferences should be considered and informed removes some of the simplicity and theoretical appeal of the preference theory of welfare. Whether this means the theory should be given up depends on a number of factors. Some might say that welfare just *is* complex, and that the complexity of any theory of it is therefore not a weakness. Some supporters may feel that they can explain what right, sensibly weighted information is. And other moves, within the broad boundaries of preference theory, are no doubt possible.

The truth is that each of the leading theories of welfare has its own problems, so in the end the question may be about which theory has the fewest shortcomings. In the discussion above we have seen, in effect, that none of the theorists we have considered is very clearly in a position to claim this distinction yet. Yes, qualitative hedonism of Mill's kind deals well with problems raised by Benthamite hedonism. Yes, an objective list of the ingredients of welfare offers a reply to the experience machine argument that is denied to hedonists. And yes, the preference theory is appealing because it is simpler than an objective list and relieves us of the far from straightforward task of actually compiling and defending a list. But the attentive reader will have spotted that we are approaching a circular argument.

Let us agree for argument's sake that some preference satisfactions add to an individual's welfare and others don't. Someone is bound to ask now: which, and why? When we try to answer these questions hedonism and perfectionism are poised to re-enter the picture. If we decide that the preferences that matter are those whose satisfaction gives rise to joy and pleasure, also in the long run, the hedonist will say: "Why not just admit that it is enjoyment, or pleasure, that matters?" If we opt for preferences associated with wholesome activities we approve of (friendship, not drug addiction) the perfectionist will cry out: "Why not just admit that these activities are what matter?"

However welfare is defined, the next step is to work out the relationship between it and ethical questions about what, morally, we are permitted or obliged to do. Thus we might wonder: Is the advancement of welfare the only thing that matters from an ethical point of view? If not, how should we balance welfare against other values and concerns? This will be discussed in some of the following chapters.

Key points

- The aim of this chapter was to discuss what welfare is and how it matters. The starting point was the view that what matters is the prevention of pain and other forms of negative welfare. Some have argued that, ethically speaking, our only concern should be to avoid negative welfare and that we need not promote positive welfare. However, it was argued that this position is paradoxical.

- The next step in the attempt to define welfare was hedonism, which can be interpreted either as a psychological theory about what in fact motivates us or as a normative theory about what makes one life go better than another. The focus here was on normative hedonism: a theory which claims that the only thing that improves well-being is pleasure (and possibly other positive mental states) and the avoidance of pain (and possibly other negative mental states).

- Two criticisms of this view were discussed. The first was that pleasures are qualitatively different. The simple, classical presentation of hedonism fails to account for this. The other was that we seem to care about things other than our mental states – for instance, we want to actually achieve things, not merely to have the experience of achievement.

- Taking up the second of these points, we touched briefly on the objective list theory of well-being. This theory seems to "fit the data" well enough. On the other hand, however, quite what should go on the list is always likely to be controversial. Moreover, the list view it is arguably lacking in the kind of simplicity and explanatory power generally sought in a theory; and moreover it is difficult to see how one can define a list that could be universally accepted.

- In light of these criticisms the proposal that a person's welfare consists in the satisfaction of his or her preferences was considered at length. This proposal has a number of clear advantages. For one thing it appears simple. It also seems to be explanatorily powerful, and it blends well with modern liberal political and economic theory. On the other hand, the proposal appears to need a rather important addition: it must be qualified by the requirement that preferences are considered and informed. Unfortunately this introduces its own difficulties, and reduces what appeared to be its great virtue, simplicity.

- The concept of well-being seems to be both elusive and contestable. None of the candidate theories of welfare presented in this chapter can be said to be obviously right: each comes with advantages and disadvantages.

References

Bentham, Jeremy (1830): *The Rationale of Reward*. London: Robert Heward. [First published 1775-1785]

Mill, John Stuart (1863): *Utilitarianism*. London: Longmans, Green, Reader, and Dyer.

Nozick, Robert (1974): *Anarchy, state and utopia*. New York: Basic Books.

Patz, Jonathan A.; Campbell-Lendrum, Diarmid; Holloway, Tracey & Foley, Jonathan A. (2005): Impact of regional climate change on human health. *Nature* 438: 310-317.

Popper, Karl R. (1966): *The Open Society and its Enemies, Vol. 1, The Spell of Plato* (5th edition). Princeton NJ: Princeton University Press. [First published 1945]

Singer, Peter (2002): A Response to Martha Nussbaum: Reply to Martha Nussbaum, 'Justice for Non-Human Animals', *The Tanner Lectures on Human Values*, November 13, 2002.
http://www.utilitarianism.net/singer/by/20021113.htm

Smart, R.N. (1958): Negative Utilitarianism. *Mind* 67: 542-543.

Further reading

Crisp, Roger (2006): *Reasons and the Good*. Oxford: Clarendon Press.

Feldman, Fred (2004): *Pleasure and the Good Life: Concerning the Nature, Varieties, and Plausibility of Hedonism*. Oxford: Clarendon Press.

Griffin, James (1986): *Well-being: Its Meaning, Measurement and Moral Importance*. Oxford: Clarendon Press.

Kraut, Richard (2007): *What is Good and Why: The Ethics of Well-Being*. Cambridge MA: Harvard University Press.

Nussbaum, Martha & Sen, Amartya (eds.) (1993): *The Quality of Life*. Oxford: Clarendon Press.

Paul, Ellen Frankel; Miller, Fred D. Jr. & Paul, Jeffrey (eds.) (1992): *The Good Life and the Human Good*. Cambridge UK: Cambridge University Press.

Sandøe, Peter (1999): Quality of life – Three competing views. *Ethical Theory and Moral Practice* 2 (1): 11-23.

Sumner, L.W. (1996): *Welfare, Happiness, and Ethics*. Oxford: Clarendon Press.

3

More than welfare?

The reason it would be wrong to not to leave a three year-old child alone near a hot stove is that the stove presents a threat to the child's well-being. The obvious reason you are permitted to relax a little more at the soft play area is that, in that environment, the child is much less vulnerable. But is the ethical life all about promoting, or maximizing, what is good for people, and minimizing what is bad? If this were so, our ethical lives would in some ways be simple. To resolve moral issues we could focus exclusively on the things that promote and threaten welfare. However, we often find ourselves in situations where things other than well-being seem to be ethically important. Respect for the dead – even though it is impossible for them to benefit - is one example. Disapproval of lying is another. We also value the freedom to make our own choices, even when that jeopardizes our own welfare. Do the values at play in these familiar cases actually increase our welfare in the long run? Or does their importance reveal that ethics is not just about welfare?

Is welfare the *only* thing that matters when you are trying to assess whether some act or practice is ethically good or valuable, or do additional factors need to be considered? This question might at first seem rather abstract and theoretical. To see the point of it, we shall consider what would be the case if welfare really were our sole ethical consideration. Let us therefore begin by looking at the public reaction to an apparently reasonable suggestion about the disposal of corpses: that they should be cremated in ovens which are linked to, and hence heat, nearby buildings. Would this be a good thing? This is probably not a subject many of us have thought about and one which, when we start to think about it, makes many of us a bit uneasy. This became apparent in Denmark around 2005 when several city councils around the country began utilizing the excess heat from crematorium ovens in district heating systems.

The Danish minister for religious affairs at that time, Bertel Haarder, felt so uneasy that he asked the Danish Ethical Council to discuss the subject in 2006. The Council concluded that it was an acceptable practice as long as the dead body and the wishes of the deceased and the bereaved were treated with respect. The practice, it said, would create a symbolic link between the deceased individual and the processes of nature. And in the present situation, where the living are threatened by climate change linked to excessive use of fossil fuels, it would be wise to utilize the heat from the crematorium ovens in this way.

These seem to be sound, well-founded and robust practical arguments. However, in the Danish newspapers it soon became apparent that many people, though they understood the reasoning behind the Council's conclusion, felt that something was not right about the proposed practice. The Council's arguments, cogent though they were, failed to dispel public unease – arguably, for two main reasons. First, death is something most of us try to avoid thinking about. Death is inevitable, and it is frightening and normally deeply upsetting to contemplate both our own death and the death of our loved ones. The other reason, and the more important one here, is that, intuitively, it seems disrespectful to utilize the earthly remains of our loved ones in this way. The practice may be good for the environment and economical, but a straightforward focus on practical benefits of this kind is, in the face of death, taboo. The value of respect for the deceased (and their mourners) seems to outweigh such mundane considerations.

In saying this we are not declaring agreement with those who object to this way of using heat from cremations. Rather, the purpose of the illustration is to highlight a case in there is widespread unease about a benefits-driven decision.

A note before we proceed: we aim still in this chapter to focus on discussions of what ultimately *matters*, ethically speaking, *good versus bad*, and to postpone to the next section discussions about how to balance things in decisions on what to do, *right versus wrong*. As we have said, some believe that only welfare matters, in its own right. The present chapter concerns whether this is really so. Some believe that certain acts, attitudes, distributions matter in their own right and not just because of consequences for welfare. For instance, some believe that taking a life is *bad* –because of the consequences for welfare. In contrast to this, some believe that killing is always *wrong* (not "merely" something bad that can be balanced against other concerns). On certain conceptions of morality – by no means them all – this means that the boundary between *what matters* (the good) and *what is right and wrong* (the right) is less clear than what we in general try to convey. If we sometimes overstep the line between discussions of the good and discussions of the right, it is a reflection of such theories.

The truth, the whole truth and nothing but the truth – so help me, God!

For most of us being honest is important. We consider it to be ethically important, that we tell the truth. Honesty is so fundamental to our society that the classic movie scene from an American court-room in which the witness places her or his hand on the Bible and swears to tell the truth, the whole truth and nothing but the truth has an almost iconic status. We take pride in being honest. We are ashamed to be caught twisting the truth, and few things provoke as much outrage in us as being unfairly accused of being a liar. Look at the pain in a child's eyes when he or she is wrongly disbelieved, or think of your own sense of self-righteousness when you have spoken truly but are treated as a liar.

This does not mean, however, that we never condone lying. We may do this, for example, where the lie benefits someone else – perhaps it is a kindness – although even here the liar usually feels the need to justify his or her actions by pointing to benefits and proving that something good was accomplished. It goes without saying that few of us feel the need to do the same when we tell the truth. Truths seem to carry their own justification.

Generally, then, we value that people tell the truth. But why is it so? Is it because honesty is intrinsically valuable? Or is truth-telling a habit we approve of because in the long run our collective interests are served by it – because honesty oils the wheels of personal and societal interaction? The first of these options seems to take us away from the idea that ethics is all about welfare. The second brings us back to that idea.

Lying about sex

Is infidelity a bad thing? Most would say that it is – at least, when their partner is present. At the same time we know from social studies that it is quite common. But why should one not lie to one's partner about sexual liaisons? An answer that many would reach for is that being unfaithful *hurts* others – your partner and perhaps your children, or your wider family. Is that correct? But is that the only reason – and does that mean that it is ethically acceptable to cheat on your partner as long as no one loses any welfare because of it? (We here assume that this is a possibility although that might be disputed).

Before discussing this, we need to make a few observations. We humans have an almost devilish ability to reconstruct reality around us so that doing what benefits ourselves the most also seems to be the most beneficial thing to do for everyone involved. We are experts at lying to ourselves and others in order to cast ourselves in a positive light. The divide between people's ideals and actions can sometimes be surprisingly wide. And we can be very persistent in our efforts to deny this when it is brought to our attention.

Let us now consider some specific cases and see whether they change our intuitive understanding of infidelity. Let us imagine that the liaison was an unmemorable fling which left the cheat feeling full of remorse and guilt and something that he or she would never do again. What if the relationship in the background is otherwise stable and there are several children involved, so that telling the truth might cause more harm than burying the whole miserable affair? Here, should the truth be told, no matter what? Or should the cheat take all the circumstances into account before deciding what to do? Lying, or keeping quiet, would spare all involved a great deal of misery. Is that good enough reason to lie?

Remember the old saying *what you don't know cannot hurt you*. Let us imagine that the cheat can, by being dishonest, not only save his or her own skin, but also the relationship. It may well be that the deceived partner will have a better life if he or she is not told about what has taken place. Against this, some will feel that using honesty and dishonesty simply as tools to promote welfare is problematic. They will claim that dishonesty is inherently wrong and ethically unjustifiable, whatever the reasons.

What we think about this situation varies from person to person depending on our values and our interpretation of the situation at hand. In the discussion above we have not argued that one should always be faithful, and always tell one's partner the truth. We have certainly not attempted to nail down the many factors settling these issues. Our key point is just that the ethical issues raised by infidelity and the lies that often accompany it may require us to think beyond welfare – to consider factors other than the impact of our actions on well-being. The difference between faithfulness and unfaithfulness, and between lying and telling the truth, may have an inherent ethical importance: that this is so is suggested by the curious phenomenon that we usually feel the need to justify our lies – not our truths. Initially, then, it seems that fidelity and honesty are more than tools for creating welfare: they appear to be ethically relevant in their own right.

White lies and merciful lies

Although there is a temptation to think initially that the truth is important in itself, after deeper reflection we may end up taking a *welfarist* approach and hold that the reason we consider the truth to be important is that it tends to generate more well-being than lying (a "welfarist" is someone who believes that, ultimately, welfare is all that matters, ethically speaking). This might lead us to formulate a rule about lying along these lines: in general, we ought to tell the truth, but in some situations the welfare impacts are such that we are permitted, or even ethically obliged, to tell a lie.

We label some permissible lies "white lies", but what exactly makes a lie white? This question turns out to be more complex than it looks. Pretty clearly, white lies tend to have a relatively limited *impact* on the world: generally they benefit the liar a little, and impose only a smallish cost or burden on the person being lied to. Sometimes the lie is even told to protect the other. But this is not the whole story. Some kinds of subject matters seem to impose a stronger demand on us to tell the truth than others. Lies about one's identity tend to be more serious than lies about the traffic on the way to work. Some relationships, likewise, require more of us as truth-tellers. By and large most of us experience that it is worse to tell a lie to our best friend than it is to tell the same lie to a member of the cabin crew on a long-haul flight. So as well as having low impacts, white lies seem to involve departures from the truth which are, for various reasons, *unimportant*.

White lies serve an important social function. They allow us to get along when some kind of social disharmony is in the offing: "So good of you to come", "I love your new hairstyle", "thanks for the meal, it was delicious" – all are familiar white lies. Here, lies are a necessary part of the social matrix, a kind of glue which enables us to behave in a civilized manner in situations in which telling the truth may create friction and perhaps hurt others.

So, although most of us would agree that, in general, lying is not ethically commendable, we nonetheless accept that there are situations in which we perhaps ought to lie. To some, these situations are those in which the liar has something to gain by lying, but to most of us, lying is acceptable only where it benefits someone else. Someone who's well-being would be damaged by the truth. The notion of a "merciful lie" is founded on this reasoning. The fourth-century theologian Saint Augustine (354–430) considered merciful lies to be among the very few cases of an evil being permissible because it prevents a greater evil.

> *If a sick man should ask a question which it is not expedient that he should know, and might be even more grievously afflicted even by thy*

returning him no answer, wilt thou venture either to tell the truth to the destruction of the man's life, or rather hold thy peace, than by a virtuous and merciful lie to be serviceable to his health. (Augustine. Quoted from Jackson (2001), p. 55)

Augustine himself seems to be in some doubt here. He has a very hard time accepting that some lies are ethically acceptable, but he cannot avoid the conclusion that the merciful lie might be preferable at times. Actually this issue remains relevant today, even though Augustine lived almost 1700 years ago. In today's hospitals the principles of autonomy (giving the patient the right to accept or decline care) and informed consent (giving the patient the right to all information about his or her disease, so that any decisions are fully informed) are sacrosanct. No doctor would openly withhold important information from a patient, or openly prevent a patient from making important decisions based on her own values.

But is it always right to tell patients how serious their condition is? Once, when the relationship between doctors and patients was based on the patriarchal authority of the doctor, it was common practice for a doctor to tell the patient whatever the doctor felt would benefit the patient the most – which was not always the truth. For example, it was regarded as cruel to tell people there was no hope left.

That Augustine – a lucid, elaborate thinker with an instinctive conviction that we should never lie – stumbled here and became rather apologetic should not surprise us. He is just expressing what most of us feel when faced with this kind of dilemma. Sometimes we do feel morally obliged to do something that we would otherwise consider wrong. As an American committee on bioethics put it when asked to discuss the ethical implications of the cloning of human cells for therapeutic purposes:

Finally, we must proceed with the paradox that accompanies all human suffering and human imperfection in full view: that sometimes we seem morally obligated to do morally troubling things, and that sometimes doing what is good means living with a heavy heart in doing it. (The President's Council on Bioethics 2002, p. 140)

A rigorous German who admitted no exceptions

We seem to be taking one step forward and two steps back in our attempt to gain an understanding of the relationship between telling the truth and lying. In some instances, lying seems ethically justifiable, but at the same time it is hard to question the pleasingly simple view that telling the truth is what we are required to do ethically. What we can say is that honesty is important. Otherwise lying would be considered unproblematic.

Admittedly, this is not a very clear position to take. The advantage of it is that it enables us to take the complex social context of our lives into account. This advantage is off-set by what some would feel to be a serious disadvantage: in this way of thinking we have no clear and uncomplicated rule on truth-telling and the inherent wrongness of lying disappears. The eighteenth-century German philosopher Immanuel Kant (1724–1804) – one of the greatest thinkers in western philosophy – famously had a much more rigorous attitude to lying. He believed that it is always wrong and can never be excused, no matter what the situation.

Kant was particularly suspicious of the way we allow self-interest to shape the way we conceive a situation. We twist situations to our own advantage by inventing excuses for lying. We say we are helping others when in fact this masks our true intention, which is to take care of our own interests. Kant saw this tendency as a dangerous form of corruption:

> *If necessity is urged as an excuse, it might be urged to justify stealing, cheating and killing and the whole basis of morality goes by the board. Then again, what is a case of necessity? Everybody will interpret it in his own way and, as there is no definite standard to judge by, the application of moral rules becomes uncertain.* (Kant. Quoted from Jackson (2001), p. 56)

For Kant there are several reasons why honesty is an absolute moral duty. The most important is that the principle that lying is permitted is self-contradictory and cannot be universalized. Very roughly, what Kant meant by this was that a general rule stating that lying is legitimate, or ethical, would be self-defeating and render communication between humans impossible. That an action should be able to be universalized means that it should be viewed by the one who prescribes the action as obligatory for everyone in a similar situation – or a situation that does not differ in any moral relevant way – to act in the same way.

Quite generally, universalizability is the trademark of morality, according to Kant. This can be understood in several ways, but here we require only two definitions. So, universalizability is (1) a criterion of the moral that makes lying logically inconsistent and (2) a safeguard against the egoism that Kant feared would pervade ethical actions if exceptions to rules were permitted. By insisting that any action by the individual should be replicable by all, Kant is attempting to nullify the human tendency to make selfish exceptions to rules for one's own benefit.

Additionally, Kant sees lying as a denial of our humanity. It is a hallmark of human existence that we, unlike non-human animals, do not merely follow our desires. We also have the ability to critically evaluate our desires rationally. Therefore, the ability to tell the truth and resist the temptation to lie, even when a few falsehoods might help us achieve our goals, is part of being human. In this sense lying amounts to a denial of one's own and others' humanity: it diminishes both the liar and those he or she deceives.

It is worth emphasizing that for Kant even the smallest lie is prohibited. There are no exceptions at all. This became very clear when the Swiss philosopher Benjamin Constant (1767–1830) challenged Kant's claim that it would be wrong to lie about the whereabouts of an innocent friend when asked by a man who is out to murder that friend. Even in a situation like this, in which every fibre in one's body say you should lie, Kant remains resolute. Lying to the murderer would obviously be beneficial for the potential victim of the murderer, but mankind as a whole would suffer. (We should understand "suffer" here in some metaphorical sense.) *Every* act of lying, including this one, treats those you deceive as less than human. Lies *always* require you to treat others as mere tools furthering what you want to do – as Kant puts it, as means, rather than ends, in themselves.

Amazingly, to the modern reader, Kant does not even grant that one has a right to remain *silent* when asked questions like the one above. One is obliged to tell the truth, plain and simple, and there can be no refuge in a refusal to say anything at all.

On Kant's view, then, all human beings are rational and must be treated as ends, not means. To treat another person as a means to your own ends is to deny the rationality of that other person. By implication, Kant says, one is denying the rationality of human beings in general, because we are equal in the sense that all of us possess rationality. Kant goes on to say: "To be truthful (honest) in all declarations is therefore a sacred unconditional command of reason, and not to be limited by any expediency." (Kant 1889, on a Supposed Right to Tell Lies From Benevolent Motives)

We have seen that truth can be looked at in many ways. At one end of the scale it is a neutral tool. It is useful for achieving what *is* important ethically, especially well-being, but it has no ethical importance in itself. At the other end of the scale it is something valued so highly that failing to tell the truth involves denying the rationality, and indeed humanity, of human beings. Most of us hold a view somewhere between these two extremes. Like Saint Augustine, we might struggle with the idea that it is permissible to lie in order to do good. On the other hand, unlike Kant, we can imagine circumstances in which it would surely be legitimate to tell a lie. We seem to believe that telling the truth is valuable in itself, but that in certain situations other values might need to be protected, or honoured, or furthered more. We accept, in short, that the value of truth can sometimes be traded for pay-offs in other areas.

Observations of a similar kind can be made about another thing we seem to value highly: freedom, or personal liberty. The next section explains why.

Freedom

Freedom is a central concept in modern ethics. Today, in western democracies, there is very widespread agreement that people have the right to live their lives exactly as they wish as long as their choices do not harm other people in certain ways. There is a powerful consensus, in other words, that you can do what you want unless that happens to be something injurious to others. A few qualifications are needed here, as always. The most obvious is that it is not necessary for the activity at issue to actually harm another. A substantial *risk* that it will do so is often enough. Driving on the wrong side of the road is prohibited not because it always injures others, but because it has a very high probability of doing so. It presents a serious risk to others. Another point is that not all harmful activity is prohibited. If people decide to engage in an activity, like boxing or rugby, which carries an obvious risk of injury, they may do so, because they are presumed to have *consented* to the risks involved. Again, various provisos hover in the background at this point: we generally insist that the people involved are adults, of sound mind, are not under duress, and so forth. But we can leave these subtleties to one side for the time being.

Being free does not mean that your decisions are not influenced by anyone or anything. All of us have been influenced by our upbringing. We didn't choose how we were brought up. We didn't agree to the values our parents instilled in us. And there is absolutely no doubt that our experiences and lessons on how to behave during childhood affect the decisions we make as adults. However, this doesn't deprive us of freedom: we can critically evaluate our upbringing and, to some extent at least, decide whether we wish to live by these values, or reject them.

Equally, however, some "influences" on our lives do limit our freedom. If I am physically threatened, and as a consequence do something I would not normally do, such as stealing a car, I am denied freedom of choice. The influences that undermine freedom and those which don't are not always easily separated. Consider people that join a religious cult and then lose touch with friends and family. Perhaps they joined freely enough. Perhaps later they are not really free to leave. We

41

might find it very hard to say at what point their freely taken decision to become a member of the cult dispossessed them of their personal liberty. However, most of us accept that, however the lines are eventually drawn, there is a difference between being forced to steal and join a cult – between acceptable influence and coercion.

It would probably be agreed that, on the whole, liberty generates welfare. The freedom to make important decisions about education, marriage, job, children, and so on, makes life better. But is freedom valuable solely because it improves your well-being? Or does it have independent value – that is, is it intrinsically valuable. What happens when the choices we make don't increase, but rather endanger, our welfare? How important is freedom then from an ethical point of view? Let us consider a specific case.

Smoking

Smoking obviously raises questions of welfare. The impact of smoking is felt by three parties: the smokers themselves, who may develop serious diseases as a result of their habit; non-smokers in the vicinity, who smoke "passively" and may also develop serious diseases as a result; and the general population, which has to fund the healthcare smokers and passive smokers require. At the same time, however, smoking raises questions about the right of the individual to do as he or she pleases. It is therefore a good case to illustrate the complexity of the idea of freedom. In considering this case we are asking, in effect: to what extent are societies entitled, in the name of welfare, to infringe on people's freedom to pursue the activities they enjoy?

As we have hinted at earlier, there was a time when smoking in public spaces was acceptable. Restaurants, trains and cinemas, even hospital waiting rooms, were full of smokers. Children made ashtrays out of clay for their parents in kindergarten. Things have changed, obviously, and in most western countries today smoking is more or less prohibited other than outdoors and in private homes. The position has changed because today the health risks associated with smoking and passive smoking are taken to outweigh the liberty enjoyed by smokers to puff away as they please. Very few would deny that smoking is unhealthy.

Why hasn't smoking simply been banned, period? Why are smokers allowed to jeopardize their own health? We suggest that this is because most of us would consider an outright ban on smoking to be at the cost of something many consider valuable. It should be possible for someone to value the joy of smoking to the degree where it threatens his or her health as long as others health is not in danger. So far, at least, we

42

haven't banned bungee-jumping, fast food and water-skiing, although all of these activities can be hazardous to participants. A ban on smoking outright, like the imposition of a prohibition on bungee-jumping, would meddle in peoples' lives and therefore have bad consequences.

Like honesty, then, freedom to do as one sees fit seems to be something we value even though it does not always increase our welfare: it is something that should not be limited without good reason. And sometimes respect for personal freedom seems to be demanded even where placing more restrictions on peoples' choices may result in higher welfare. On the other hand, it may well be that in the future the health interests of the public and costs to health services will be appealed to in an attempt to justify further restrictions on the freedom of smokers. The idea that strongly addictive activities like smoking are not done freely anyway might be highlighted in this development. Perhaps restrictions on alcohol and unhealthy food will follow on a similar basis.

There seem to be three positions in the smoking debate. The first is that smoking is a personal choice and people should be allowed to do it as long as this doesn't affect others adversely. At the other end of the spectrum we find the opinion that smoking is not an exercise of personal freedom, since smokers are essentially drug addicts, unable to control their behaviour in a rational way. Smoking should be banned. Help can be provided for smokers to lead better lives!

Western societies seem to opt for a position somewhere between these two. Smoking is prohibited in public areas because it damages the health of others, cigarettes are taxed to make them less attractive, and public campaigns are launched to inform the public about the dangers of smoking – but the individual's choice to smoke is not interfered with. From a welfarist perspective, a total ban on smoking might increase welfare in the short run, but it risks creating a "black market", with cigarettes becoming part of organized crime, thereby reducing societal welfare in the long. Those who think that welfare is the key, or the only, thing that matters in ethical disputes will need to balance such considerations before passing judgment on what should be done. Such a weighing of the pros and cons could very well lie behind smoking policies in the western societies where you can still smoke, if you want to, although in fewer and fewer places and at a higher and higher cost.

New research has put this compromise to the test, since it has shown that approximately 10% of the dangerous ultra-fine particles in the smoke from cigarettes can drift from one apartment to another in a residential block. Thus even where there are no open doors or windows, you can still be smoking passively, if your neighbour chooses to smoke in his or her private home.

Does this mean that smoking in private homes ought to be banned in apartment blocks? Some will say this is an intolerable infringement of the freedom of the individual. To others it may seem natural to increase the protection of the public against passive smoking in this manner. In the USA a comprehensive ban on smoking is already in place in some buildings with private homes (e.g. in Seattle and New York). The U.S. Department of Housing and Urban Development is strongly encouraging city authorities around the country to ban smoking in public housing units:

> *Because Environmental Tobacco Smoke (ETS) can migrate between units in multifamily housing, causing respiratory illness, heart disease, cancer, and other adverse health effects in neighboring families, the Department is encouraging PHAs to adopt non-smoking policies. By reducing the public health risks associated with tobacco use, this notice will enhance the effectiveness of the Department's efforts to provide increased public health protection for residents of public housing.* (U.S. Department of Housing and Urban Development 2009)

Here the non-smoking policy is justified by pointing to the danger others are exposed to through passive smoking. It remains to be seen whether smoking will be banned outright, even when it poses no danger to anyone other than the smoker himself.

Is the idea that western societies will in due course impose a total ban on smoking, protecting smokers from themselves, so very far-fetched? Certainly, parallels can be pointed to. Thus in many countries the selling of one's own internal organs (e.g. kidneys) is illegal. Similarly, certain drugs are banned, as is prostitution. The extent to which these analogies really tell against smoking is debatable. However, in the cases mentioned we do appear to be protecting individuals from their own choices. Is that ethically acceptable? How much weight does well-being carry in the ethical arena? Is your well-being sufficiently important to legitimize a state ban on your doing something you are freely choosing to do?

Freedom for the not so free

In care homes for those who have lost the ability to take care of themselves as a result of dementia, the nurses and other employees face a recurring problem. The difficulty is that the residents sometimes leave the home, become lost, and cannot find their way back. In the past it was necessary to lock the outer doors to prevent residents from leaving, or in some cases to search for them when they wandered off. Today, residents who leave the premises can easily be located using a simple GPS tracking device. This gives residents more freedom of movement. It also allows the staff to treat them more like adult human beings and less like children.

These tracking devices are often tightly regulated. In many countries the use of a GPS tracking device requires written consent from the care home resident's next of kin and official approval from the social authorities. But why is this case when there is such a clear benefit, not only for the individual who is suffering from dementia, but also for the people taking care of their needs? It is presumably because the GPS involves restricting the personal freedom of an individual. There is a fine line between using such technology responsibly to improve the care of people suffering from dementia, on the one hand, and using it to control patients in a way that is potentially unethical, on the other. The dilemma is thus between the safety and the freedom of the patient – here expressed as the basic freedom of movement.

The question here is not whether the right to freedom should trump safety every time, or vice versa. Our aim is simply to present a case in which ethics gives every appearance of involving more than just welfare. Cases like these are difficult to account for, if one believes that in ethics only welfare counts. On the other hand, perhaps each and every one of the cases we have discussed in this chapter can be explained in terms of welfare, and that our feeling that ideals like truth and freedom are valuable and important in their own right is a misunderstanding. We will continue this debate in the next chapter, where we will discuss the moral status of animals, plants and nature as a whole. Here, again, we shall see that although welfare is an important ethical concept, there are various situations in which it seems that it is not the only thing that matters.

Key points

- Within ethics there is an on-going discussion about the importance of welfare. To some, the welfarists, it is the only thing that counts when ethically evaluating an action, while, to others it is just one factor among several others. Examples of values whose ethical importance may be independent of welfare include: respect for others, dignity, honesty, and freedom or autonomy. The question is whether our positive attitude to these ideals reflects the fact that we invest them with intrinsic value or the fact that they have a favourable (possibly indirect and long-term) impact on our welfare.

- In this chapter, we have discussed three examples: utilizing human remains as biofuel, lying and limiting the personal freedom of individuals. In all three cases, welfare considerations are important, but there also seems to be something else at stake. In the case of lying, even if a lie might save a relationship that is worth saving and make everyone involved better off than they would be if they were presented with the ugly truth, we still seem to feel that the lie is problematic. Thus the view that lying is a neutral tool that can be used effectively to create welfare seems to go against some deeply held ethical intuitions. On the other hand, the opposing, and extreme, view that one may never lie suffers from the difficulties itself. Sometimes situations are configured in a way that strongly suggests that lying is the right thing to do – or, at least, the lesser of two evils.

- Similar remarks apply to the other two cases. From a welfarist perspective the reason why we should protect the freedom of individuals, tell the truth and treat the dead with respect is that this kind of behaviour cultivates welfare. But many of us believe that we do not tell the truth merely because it will eventually lead to the best outcome. We do so because we find it valuable to do so regardless of the consequences. It is not easy to decide who is right. As we have seen, quite a number of considerations can be adduced in support of either position.

References

Jackson, Jennifer (2001): *Truth, Trust and Medicine*. London & New York: Routledge.

The President's Council on Bioethics (2002): *Human Cloning and Human Dignity: An Ethical Inquiry*. Washington DC: The President's Council on Bioethics.

Kant, Immanuel (1889): *Kant's Critique of Practical Reason and Other Works on the Theory of Ethics* (translated by Thomas Kingsmill Abbott, 4th revised edition). London, New York & Bombay: Longmans, Green and Co. [First published 1785-1797]. Accessed from http://oll.libertyfund.org/title/360/61937/642114 on 23 August 2013

U.S. Department of Housing and Urban Development: *Non-Smoking Policies in Public Housing* (NOTICE: PIH-2009- 21 (HA)). Washington DC.

Further reading

Bok, Sissela (1989): *Lying. Moral Choice in Public and Private Life*. New York: Vintage Books. [First published 1978]

Goodin, Robert E. (1989): The ethics of smoking. *Ethics* 99 (3): 574-624.

Kagan, Shelly (1998): *Normative Ethics*. Boulder CO: Westview Press.

Tännsjö, Torbjörn (2002): *Understanding ethics: An Introduction to Moral Theory*. Edinburgh: Edinburgh University Press Ltd.

4

What about nature?

So far we have been discussing issues about what matters arising from our dealings with one another and the regulation of those dealings by the state. In this chapter we will discuss what happens when nature is brought into the debate. Should we value nature simply because, in the end, this is in our own interests, or are we also obliged to consider nature for its own sake? The question of how far the ethical community extends beyond the human boundary is central in any discussion of how nature should be treated. This chapter introduces the four main ethical positions adopted in the discipline of environmental ethics. It also asks what exactly is meant by the term "nature". Is there an ethical difference between wild, untouched nature and the habitats, animals and plants that have been cultivated and adapted in various ways down through the millennia – should farmed pigs and wild boars be treated differently? Finally, we discuss the many ethical conflicts and dilemmas that arise when the ethical community is expanded beyond the human sphere.

Somewhere not far from the North Pole stands a bewildered polar bear. What confuses this furry giant is that its prey, the seal pup, is lying on the ice with its mother close by. Usually, the pup would be in a snow cave dug out by its mother, invisible to its enemies. The polar bear has to search around, sniffing its way to the cave. And when it finds the cave, it has to break in to get to the seal pup. On this occasion, the snow is too shallow and too soft for the seal mother to dig a cave for its pup. Climate change has put an end to this kind of parental protection, and the seal is forced to raise its pup out in the open. Contrary to appearances, this is not an advantage for the polar bear. It is so brilliantly designed to hunt using its olfactory sense that now it is at a loss as to what to do. The seals, mother and pup, can see the bear approaching. They have plenty of time to slide into the water and make their escape.

From a purely evolutionary point of view this is nothing new. It is the way evolution works. The environment changes and organisms are forced to either adapt and survive or become extinct. After all, the polar bear was originally a brown bear or grizzly that got caught by glaciers in the mid-Pleistocene age somewhere between 100 and 250 thousand years ago. Thus, the polar bear will have to adapt to a more terrestrial life style, or be replaced by its old relatives in the new arctic environment that is developing. If we strip the problem down to its basic scientific components, it is doubtful whether there are any ethical questions at stake here. What we have is just a natural phenomenon unfolding, although one can obviously discuss whether human-induced climate change can be described as natural.

However, to most people there is more than science to the world. The experience of the polar bear – although usually seen from a safe distance on the TV – and the symbolic importance of the animal, together with the images of polar bears clinging to melting pieces of ice in an immense ocean, carry an ethical component: a feeling of wrongness and perhaps even guilt, and an urge to do something – although few of us actually get around to this before we get caught up in the daily trivialities of our lives once more, far away from the melting ice and the hungry polar bears.

What is important?

In this chapter we shall extend the discussion of what matters beyond the human sphere to include the rest of nature. In the case of the polar bear it is arguably obvious that one can extend the debate and ask whether it is ethically acceptable that human greenhouse gas emissions are damaging an animal's welfare. Few in the western world, at any rate, would deny that mammals have welfare of a kind that can be neglected or nurtured, and that this fact should be taken into consideration by us – although we might argue about the extent to which animal welfare matters. But what about animals like shrimps and spiders? What about plants? Do trees, flowers and mosses, for example, have moral standing? And how should we regard non-living things such as mountains, rivers and ecosystems. Can and should they be included in the ethical community somehow?

Climate change raises many questions of a scientific nature. But it also raises new ethical issues, and it emphasizes old questions in new ways. One obvious question to ask in this connection is: why should I care? Is it because it is wrong for people not to care about polar bears? Should we care because it is wrong that an individual polar bear loses its life, or because it is wrong to destroy an animal species? Alternatively, does causing such a drastic change on an ecosystem constitute a loss of value in itself? Or is it that I should only care if, in some sense, other people would be harmed if the polar bear were to disappear from the face of the Earth? These are not easy questions. They require us to consider our fundamental understanding of the natural world and our relationship as human beings to that world.

Complex though they may be, these questions have been discussed within philosophy and theology throughout human history, but they moved to the forefront of ethical thinking with the advent of the ecological crisis in the 1960s and growing public awareness of environmentalism as a political subject. Since the 1970s such issues have given birth to the environmental movement and a new academic discipline: *environmental ethics.*

One approach to the kinds of question this discipline works with is to look at the ways in which different arguments can be used to support different understandings of the ethical importance of non-human nature. In the following we will describe the four main positions within environmental ethics and discuss some of the strengths and weaknesses of each. If we for a moment return to the example of the polar bear, the importance of this discussion should be clear: The resources we should allocate to preserving the polar bear and the priority the issue should be given in the current situation in which climate change threatens human lives in many parts of the world depends on how we ethically evaluate the polar bear. If the only reason for saving the polar bear is our own aesthetic preferences, we will probably not prioritize the preservation of the animal very highly, whereas if we believe that it is a creature that has ethical importance in itself, we may well consider its preservation to be very important.

Agents, subjects and objects

Let us begin by dividing everything in the world into three groups. The first consists of ethical *agents*. Ethical agents are able to understand and act on the basic ideas of ethics as laid out in this book. They therefore have ethical obligations, and we are justified in expecting them to meet these obligations. An ethical agent can be held accountable for his or her actions. Alien creatures could be ethical agents, of course, and there is arguably rudimentary ethical behaviour within the animal world (e.g. among chimpanzees and dolphins), but in a rough and ready way we can assume that all ethical agents are human.

Ethical agents are at the same time ethical *subjects*. As well as having ethical obligations, they should be treated ethically – they deserve moral consideration. Ethical subjects are those which ethical

49

agents have obligations towards. This means that ethical agents are obliged to take the interests and preferences of ethical subjects into consideration when deciding what to do. Ethical subjects have ethical importance in themselves. They have *moral standing.* It is widely accepted, however, that some ethical subjects are not ethical agents. Think of children, those with mental impairment (e.g. dementia), people in comas, and so on. As illustrated in the figure below, this means that ethical agents are a sub-group of the larger group of ethical subjects.

The final group comprises ethical *objects.* These have no ethical importance in themselves – they are not ethical subjects, in other words. Nor, obviously, are they ethical agents. However, ethical agents may still have to take ethical objects into consideration, because failure to do so could have an impact on someone or something that *does* merit consideration, i.e. an ethical subject. Very few people would take a beautiful vase to be an ethical subject. Therefore the act of destroying the vase is not ethically wrong in itself. However, this act may be wrong because of the effect it has on the owner of the vase – because it upsets someone needlessly, say. By contrast, one might consider flowers to be ethical subjects of a kind that are to be taken into consideration for their own sake. Perhaps causing their death by picking them in order to display them in a vase would be ethically objectionable. They might be very rare, for example.

Together ethical agents and subjects constitute what we shall call the *ethical community.* Ethical objects are not members of this community. In our classification they are only relevant in so far as their presence or absence, and condition, affects the members.

The ethical community

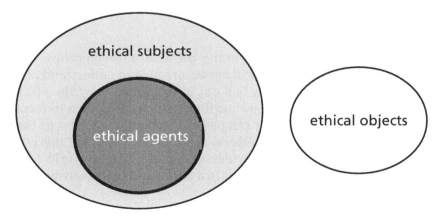

If we deploy this conceptual scheme to organize the debate within environmental ethics, the overarching question becomes one about membership. That is, what kinds of entity or living thing belong to each category? Membership of the ethical agent category is relatively uncontroversial. It is basically us, human beings, or at least those human beings with the mental capacity to be held responsible for their actions, who are ethical agents. But the boundaries of the other two, non-overlapping categories are more debatable. Where do the margins of these groups lie?

In essence there are four positions here. The *anthropocentric* position is that only humans get into the ethical subjects category – that only humans have moral standing. Everything else is an ethical object. The *sentientist* (or zoocentric) view is that all sentient beings, including many non-human animals, are ethical subjects. Animals lacking sentience, and of course plants and rocks, are mere objects, ethically speaking. The *biocentric* position includes all living beings, including plants, in the group of ethical subjects. Finally, the *ecocentric* position adds that some non-living entities – e.g. mountains, rivers and more systemic entities such as species, ecosystems and landscapes – are ethical subjects.

Initially this moral taxonomy may seem rather academic. It is not. So much depends on whether one is considered a fully-fledged member of the ethical community or excluded from it. Consider the debate about our treatment of agricultural animals. If animals are just ethical objects, no ethical limits are placed *by the animals themselves* on our exploitation of them in the production system. So far as the animals are concerned, we are entitled to do just as we wish. If we want to produce more meat for less money, we may do so. But if animals are ethical subjects, they are beings with moral importance and they should be treated accordingly in agricultural production systems. Then there are limits to how much pressure we can exert on animals to reach our own goals.

In the next four sections we shall put the fourfold moral taxonomy just described to work. We begin with the most conservative option: anthropocentrism.

Us and them *par excellence* – anthropocentrism

Anthropocentrism (from the Greek *anthropos* = man) is the view that only humans can be ethical subjects. It finds support in main-stream interpretations of Western religion, and for centuries it was an almost self-evident fact within Western philosophy. It does not mean that animals, plants and the environment are morally invisible, of course. The position is rather that ethical consideration for *anything* other than humans is always indirect, and ultimately based on human needs and interests.

The anthropocentric attitude appears to inform the 1987 UN report 'Our Common Future' – the so-called Brundtland Report. This document links the need to change our behaviour towards the environment with the needs of future generations; human generations, that is! (World Commission on Environment and Development 1987). Over the past 20 years the Brundtland approach has had a significant impact on environmental and nature management – for example, in connection with energy consumption, waste policies and the protection of animal and plant species. Thus from an anthropocentric sustainability perspective the extinction of polar bears becomes interesting for a number of reasons. Polar bears feed on seals, which in turn feed on fish. Fewer polar bears would all things being equal mean more seals and fewer fish. This in turn would have a negative impact on fisheries in the regions where polar bears live, or rather lived. Local economies would suffer, adversely affecting the vulnerable human populations who depend on them. Obviously, there would be no polar bears to attract the tourists who boost local economies.

At some point advocates the anthropocentric perspective need to explain why it is only members of the species *Homo sapiens* that merit ethical consideration in and of themselves – something it has proved increasingly difficult to do. Beyond a narrow religious understanding on which human beings have been specially selected by God to have dominion over the natural world there is little enthusiasm today for simple, species-based anthropocentric positions.

The question for the anthropocentric ethicist, if he rejects the religious explanation, thus becomes: what qualities do human beings possess that elevates them – and only them – to the status of ethical subjects? Or, in plain language, what *about us* makes us special? In the recent history of moral philosophy, many different qualities have been proposed: reason or rationality, language, the ability to use tools, and so on. The problem is evident right away. Not all people possess these abilities: children, the mentally disabled and people suffering from dementia may not, for example. What about these individuals? This argument, known as *the argument from marginal cases*, has been promoted by e.g. the Australian utilitarian Peter Singer:

> *The catch is that any such characteristic that is possessed by all human beings will not be possessed only by human beings. For example, all human beings, but not only human beings, are capable of feeling pain; and while only human beings are capable of solving complex mathematical problems, not all humans can do this.* (Singer 2002, p. 237)

Another philosopher, the American John Rawls (1921–2002), answered this challenge in his influential work *A Theory of Justice* from 1971 (1999). He pointed to the *potential* for these less capable people to acquire the necessary abilities. Some of us actually have the necessary abilities. Others have had them in the past, or will do so in the future, or (more distantly still) could have had them, because they belong to the species *Homo sapiens*.

Is that convincing? Do we experience out moral life in the way Rawls says? Do we feel obligated to help the person in front of us whatever his or her capabilities or do we help, because we have the rationality to super-impose an image of the person that could been on the actual person?

Enter the animals – sentientism

Since the 1960s mankind's relationship with nature has come under closer scrutiny than ever before. Few observers, if any, today would support the anthropocentric viewpoint – especially its implication that all animals are objects with no inherent moral significance. The most serious objections to the anthropocentric stance have come from two directions. Each in its own way is *zoocentric*.

The first attack on anthropocentrism is based on the idea that what matters morally is *sentience*: the capacity to feel, experience sensations, and perceive the world through external senses such as sight and touch. This sentientist point of view is associated with hedonist welfarism. It is not hard to see why. Welfarism claims that the ethical acceptability of our actions depends solely on their impact on welfare. Hedonism claims that the individual's level of welfare is determined solely by the balance of his or her positive and negative mental states. In classical hedonism this is taken to mean the balance of pleasure over pain. It can be seen, then, that welfarist hedonism more or less automatically moves one into a sentientist position. Once this position is agreed, animals have to be brought into the moral community.

The English radical Jeremy Bentham (1748–1832), who we met in chapter 2, was very clear on how his welfarist perspective entailed a re-evaluation of the ethical stance of animals:

> *The day may come when the rest of the animal creation may acquire those rights which never could have been withholden from them but by the hand of tyranny ... Is it the faculty of reason, or perhaps the faculty of discourse [that excludes them from the moral community]? But a full-grown horse or dog is beyond comparison a more rational, as well as a more conversable animal, than an infant of a day or a week or even a month, old. But suppose they were otherwise, what*

would it avail? The question is not, Can they reason? nor, Can they talk? but, Can they suffer? Why should the law refuse its protection to any sensitive being? ... The time will come when humanity will extend its mantle over everything which breathes. (Bentham 1789, chapter XV11, note 122)

It is fair to say that animal welfare is higher on the public agenda today than at any time previously. Today, fewer persons than before would say that an animal's experience of comfort and suffering is ethically irrelevant. The really important questions concern the implications of sentientism for animal and indeed human treatment. Which animals *are* sentient? How sentient are they? Is their sentience as important, morally, as human sentience, and if not, why not? Does the sentientist perspective create difficulties for our treatment of some human beings? People unlucky enough to enter medical conditions such as deep coma and some forms of persistent vegetative state appear to be deprived of sentient experience. Does that mean their moral standing diminishes, or maybe even disappears?

Questions like the latter points to what some perceive as a disqualifying limitation inherent to sentientism: That it only evaluates the direct experience of the animal, e.g. whether the slaughter process is painful or humane and done in a way so the animal does not suffer, but does not apart from consequences on welfare find it ethically problematic that the animal is killed. In the chapter on ethics of rights we will return to this criticism.

"Trees have moral standing" – biocentrism

The notion that it is necessary to be sentient to be an ethical subject is rejected by those who see *life* as the key definer of the moral community. Advocates of this biocentric approach claim that to be an ethical subject it is sufficient to be a living thing. All living organisms – whatever their level of consciousness – are included: human beings, certainly, and animals of every kind, but also plants.

One of the first modern academic works to explore the possibilities of biocentrism was written by Christopher D. Stone, an American professor of law, who discussed the moral and legal status of non-sentient entities in 1972 in *Should Trees Have Standing?* (Stone 2010). In 1986 the American environmental ethicist Paul W. Taylor published the book *Respect for Nature. A Theory of Environmental Ethics* in which he argued in favour of the biocentric perspective using the idea of "a good of its own". For Taylor the key moral issue is whether or not it makes sense to say of something – a person, an animal, a plant, or a lump of rock – that things can be good or bad for it. Can we say that some event (e.g. a rainstorm) or certain conditions (e.g. of great heat) would help or damage the thing whose moral status we are interested in? If we can, according to Taylor, the thing has a good of its own, and therefore ethical value: it is, in our terms, an ethical subject. Taylor infers that all living beings, whether fauna or flora, belong to the ethical community. Trees, bushes and vegetables are in the moral circle, and the idea that they shouldn't be is a zoocentric bias.

Other biocentric positions include the claim that, on the basis of our human experiences, the ability of humans to identify with 'the other' must be what defines the boundary of the ethical community. The limits of the ethical community are drawn by the human ability to identification. To identify with a being is also to be able to have empathy with a being. And since humans share some existential basic conditions such as vulnerability and mortality with all life forms, there is a possibility to experience empathy with all living things – and that is consequently where the line has to be drawn for the ethical community. Inanimate objects such as rocks, rivers, mountains etc. do not share basic conditions with us in the same way and thus only have indirect ethical significance (i.e. they are ethical objects).

If you forget the whole you lose the parts – ecocentrism

Although the various anti-anthropocentric perspectives we have been examining differ in many ways, they have a common feature: all focus on the *individual*, and each assumes that it is only single individuals that matters ethically. What happens to the community, whether that community is conceived in human or ecological terms, is only important because, and in so far as, it has an impact on the individual.

Supporters of a holistic approach consider the above insufficient. They insist that the ethical community can only be defined in a satisfactory way when everything in the natural world, living or dead – not just individual organisms – is considered. So-called *deep ecologists* point out that current environmental problems such as air pollution and what they consider to be the ruthless exploitation of the natural world, require rethinking our role in the natural world. According to this perspective, human exploitation of the natural world is a symptom of the fact that we have forgotten a fundamental truth: together with other living organisms, we are embedded in a larger ecosystem. Everything is interconnected. Humans are part of the natural world and are so closely associated with the rest of it that, ethically speaking, the distinction between *humans* and *nature* is utterly fruitless. The boundary of the individual is not the thin layer of skin covering the body. The individual in a certain sense *is* also all the ecological processes that it takes part in (Abram 1996).

In this vein, the Norwegian philosopher and deep ecologist Arne Næss (1912–2009) talks about the difference between the individual self and the ecological self. The latter, in a radical sense, may be understood as the ecosphere. Therefore it is not only individual organisms, but also items such as species and ecosystems, which have direct ethical significance (Naess 1989). The goal then is to preserve a high level of diversity and untouched nature and achieve a state of harmony or at least respectful disharmony between ourselves and the natural world – to make humans part of the natural cycle, so that they exist on an equal footing with other creatures and, as far as possible, avoid influencing the ecosystems more than necessary.

Aldo Leopold (1887–1948) is a leading figure in the ecocentric framework. He was an American environmentalist, ecologist and forester, whose book *A Sand County Almanac* (1949) has come to have an almost iconic status in wilderness conservation circles. In the book, Leopold attempted to identify the ideals that should inform human interaction with nature:

> *This song of the waters is audible to every ear, but there is other music in these hills, by no means audible to all. … On a still night, when the campfire is low and the Pleiades have climbed over rimrocks, sit quietly and listen … and think hard of everything you have seen and tried to understand. Then you may hear it – a vast pulsing harmony – its score inscribed on a thousand hills, its notes the lives and deaths of plants and animals, its rhythms spanning the seconds and the centuries.* (Leopold 1949, p. 158)

But what is nature?

The concept of nature shapes the different positions within environmental ethics, yet it is a concept that is notoriously difficult to define. The majority of people these days take the view that nature should be protected, but most of us would be hard pressed to say what does, and what does not, count as nature. Take city parks, created through human intervention. Should they count as nature? Why, or why not? There is a clear sense in which it isn't natural. What about old oak trees that were once planted in fields? Or animals, such as the dairy cow, that has been bred and refined by farmers for millennia? Looking at matters from the other direction, as it were, do colonies of wild rosebay willowherb on railway lines and in disused urban sites, now overgrown with weeds, form part of nature? Why not? They weren't planted, and haven't been bred or selected by us.

Perhaps we can get a grip on the concept of nature by reflecting on its opposite, or what it is replaced by: culture. Culture (from the latin *cultura* = that which is grown) is made by humans. It can take many different forms, and it can have both mental and physical qualities. Chairs are part of culture, as are democracy, astronomy, cheesecake, football and writing. Culture is produced by and for humans. Culture is the way in which humans shape the world socially, practically and ideologically.

Nature (from the latin *natura* = that which is born), by contrast, is everything that exists before humans begin to change things, to culturalize them, so to speak. It is independent of humans. It is what is given, what is there when we begin. The air is an element of nature, as are spiders, desert sand, orcas, forest strawberries and mountains.

The distinguishing feature of nature, then, seems to be that it is independent of human activity. This criterion actually works very well up to a point. It is also in keeping with the moral intuitions of many that we should respect nature and protect rare species of plant and animal, but need not accord the same respect and protection to, say, a brand of shoes.

Unfortunately things are rarely this simple. As human cultures have evolved, we have interfered and exercised power over increasingly large parts of nature. Today it is difficult to find something on the planet that is fully independent of humans. Even the most remote parts of the planet have been visited by humans, whilst chemical compounds produced and used by humans can be found in nearly all living creatures. Some effects of human pollution, such as climate change, have a significant impact on just about everything. So, in this sense, little is "natural" today.

How to deal with mixed entities?

Very often we are thinking about something other than "pure nature" when we describe something as natural. Independent nature should not necessarily be understood as that which is untouched or unaffected by humans, but as that which is whole before humans begin to change it. Nature is that which does not need us to unfold its potential. The orca, fire and forest trees would do very well without us. As a matter of fact, most living beings would flourish without humans. Here nature is seen as "the wild" or "wilderness".

Sadly, this does not solve the problem with the hybrids we have produced during the domestication process of the past millennia. Animals, such as cows, pigs, lamas and chickens, have been domesticated and bred to serve our needs. Plants have been crossed and selected so, as to be better food sources or more beautiful. In general, the agricultural sector has changed landscapes significantly, as have golf courses, paintball sites and parking lots. Nature and culture have been blended together in many different ways, and this certainly complicates matters. In the case of the parking lot it is very hard to identify any remnant of nature, whereas if we look at the Sami way of breeding reindeer the natural "part" of the animal seems easier to discern. The ordinary dairy cow sits somewhere between these two extremes.

These issues are irrelevant to the anthropocentric observer. All we have to do is makes humans better off. This sometimes means protecting non-human entities, and more specifically, natural entities, since human well-being depends on these. But the only general question we face is about how losses in the natural world affect us. Here, one can distinguish between two positions: strong and weak anthropocentrism. The former focuses solely on basic human biological needs – access to breathable air, drinkable water and edible food. The latter is broader and includes the human appetite for experiences of natural world and the possibility of bonding with other living beings. In both cases, however, the underlying ethical reasoning is that animals, plants and landscapes have value only insofar as they serve *human* interests. Whether a cow is part of nature, or culture, or a hybrid of the two, does not matter.

Likewise, the sentientist is not bothered by the vagueness of the concept of nature. In the sentientist perspective, all we need to know about a potential possessor of moral status – a dolphin, say, or a virus – is whether or not it can feel pain or if it can be considered a 'subject-of-a-life'. If it can, it is an ethical subject. If it cannot, it is ethical object and only indirectly relevant, ethically speaking. Dolphins, plainly, are capable of feeling pain and mental distress and qualify as 'subjects-of-a-life', so their well-being should be factored in when we are asking ourselves what treatment they merit. The same goes for farm animals like cattle. Viruses don't experience anything, let alone mental distress, so the sole ethical question about them is whether they are good or bad for beings that do have mental capacities – including humans and cattle, and dolphins. Whether the dairy cow – unrecognizable to its wild forebears – should be considered mostly nature or mostly culture is ethically unimportant.

Let us now turn to biocentrism. Here the independence (or rather lack of it) of the natural world can lead to surprising conclusions. Earlier, we mentioned the environmental philosopher Paul Taylor. He argues that all living beings have an ethical importance because they have *a good of their own* that is independent of humans. But, according to Taylor, this is not true of domesticated animals, because they have become so culturalized as to lose their independence. Such animals are no longer nature, but culture. This means that they cannot claim membership of the ethical community, as they are now so far from their original independent state that they have become a mere means to human ends. The cow is not so much an animal as a biological factory.

For the ecocentrist problems with the distinction between nature and culture abound. The ecocentrist tends to view cultural incursions into nature as evidence of an unnatural disturbance that threatens the ecological balance of "wild" ecosystems. But as more and more of the world ceases to be genuinely natural and takes on cultural features it becomes increasingly difficult to uphold the distinction between nature and culture. Some ecosystems, such as those that have developed around agricultural production, are not natural in the sense of being independent of human activities. But does this mean that we have no duty to take care of them? The ecocentrist answer to questions like this is that we should minimize our impact on wild nature as much as possible by designating certain zones for the production of food whilst leaving the rest as wilderness. "Step lightly on the ground" is a popular catchphrase in ecocentric circles, and one that expresses the ideal that we should leave as small an ecological footprint as possible.

Ethical dilemmas in taking care of Mother Earth

Questions about the boundaries of nature and culture are prominent in discussions of environmental protection – a subject that will only become more and more pressing, as the consequences of climate change become more apparent. What should we strive to preserve and what can we abandon? But another complex issue lies before us as well. Once we have decided what nature is, and what belongs to the ethical community, how should we go about setting priorities? It is unlikely that we will be able to live up to all of our ethical obligations to the planet at the same time.

The problem of prioritization intensifies as the scope of the ethical community grows. From an anthropocentric viewpoint only humans have ethical importance, but already here we can face situations in which we cannot choose one valuable outcome without denying another at the same time. Medical developments in organ transplantation mean that we can prolong human lives that would have been lost just a few years ago. At the same time, these developments have resulted in additional pressure and discomfort for relatives of the donor: they are faced with hard choices at the very time as they are struggling to come to terms with the death of a loved one. It is easy to imagine a situation where a hospital has a patient who is in need of an organ and whom we are technically able to help if only we can obtain an organ from a donor, and yet the relatives of a road accident victim are uncomfortable with the idea that their loved one is going to be treated as a resource.

Problems like these obviously multiply as the boundaries of the ethical community are pushed back – as more and more beings are treated as ethically relevant in themselves. We are often faced with situations in which the interests of one being clash with those of another, and where a compromise needs to be struck. Therefore, we have to decide what it is important to protect, whether we should actively meddle with nature or leave it to evolve by itself, and so on. Should we cull animals in national parks or let nature run its course and allow hunger and social herd mechanisms to ensure that animal numbers are sustainable over time? Should we conserve vast areas of potentially rich agricultural land to provide a habitat where plants and animals can continue to be part of natural evolutionary processes?

One way to answer questions like these deploys a consequentialist framework. Here the idea is that the correct course of action is the one which maximizes the welfare, or quality of life, of all those affected by it. Consequentialism (see chapter 6) has often been associated with the sentientist perspective discussed above. Because it focuses on the aggregate level of welfare, it regards individual animals merely as contributors to the overall amount of joy or suffering. Within this framework it is entirely acceptable to sacrifice the ethically relevant interests of one being as long as that leads to a larger increase of welfare somewhere else. A consequentialist would almost certainly want to argue that saving the polar bear from extinction would be extremely expensive, and that a better outcome could be achieved by using the funds to provide clean drinking water to humans in Africa. This would maximise welfare.

Another approach to prioritization would be to introduce of some kind of hierarchy of ethical importance. Usually humans, at the top of the pyramid, are deemed more important that animals, which in turn are considered more important than plants. This fits well with our intuitive sense of the relative importance of these groups, but what does it imply about the concept of a *species* and of an *ecosystem*? Where do these entities figure in the picture? Is a species more important than its individual members? Is the system more important than its components? In the early days of environmental ethics, thinkers like the American philosopher J. Baird Callicott enjoyed a degree of notoriety for maintaining that it is more important to protect ecosystemic health than it is to save humans (Callicott 1980). Deep ecologists claimed that ecological imperatives imposed a limit to the sustainable number of humans on the planet: around 250 million.

These assertions were felt to go too far, and the French philosopher Luc Ferry (1992) labelled them misanthropic. Although the criticism of these positions often misses their complexity, it remains open to question quite how we should navigate our way through an ethical landscape where beings other than humans have to be taken into consideration.

Very few of us are fanatics who would sacrifice human lives to protect nature, but many conflicts over whose interests should carry the most weight continue. Consider: the use of animals in medical experiments, the destruction of rainforests to create arable land, and the erosion of coral reefs around the world by pollutants and rising ocean temperatures that are again linked to industrial production and CO_2 emissions. There are no easy answers. Things that we care about – that which matters – tend to come into conflict and win-win situations are rarer than the win-lose situations where we have to choose among the things that we value. We will return to how this can be done in chapter 9. What is clear is that if human interests always carry the most weight when it comes to practical decision-making, talk of the *intrinsic* value of nature is bound to sound a bit hollow.

The future

The prominence of the concept of nature in ethical thinking over recent years is perhaps mainly due to two factors. First, powerful arguments have been marshalled which problematize antropocentrism and widen the ethical circle to include, in most eyes of most people, non-human animals, and more controversially plants and ecosystems. Second, industrialization and population growth around the globe has created an ecological crisis, so that we now *need* to think long and hard, both prudentially and ethically, about what we must do if we are not to destroy the natural world we know, depend on, and cherish. We hope to have shown in this chapter that the issues, and responses to them, are extremely complex. We haven't given our backing to one viewpoint, or even to one approach, not least because we, the authors, disagree strongly on this issue. We all agree whole-heartedly, however, that ethical questions about the relationship between humans and the rest of nature can only become more important in the coming years as human societies try to adapt to drastically changing living conditions.

Key points

- Our understanding of the relationship between humans and nature has become increasingly important, as anthropocentrism has lost its grip and the detrimental effects of the human activity on nature have become more severe. Pollution of the air, soil and water, the questionable levels of welfare among intensively farmed production animals and climate change are all issues that bring nature to the forefront of ethical debates.

- A fruitful way to structure the different positions in environmental ethics is to ask what kinds of thing belong in the three categories ethical *agent,* ethical *subject* and ethical *object.* Ethical agents can be held responsible for their actions. They are required to behave ethically towards ethical subjects, and a complaint can be made against them when they fail to do so. Most human beings (but not all: think of the newborn, the mentally infirm etc.) are ethical agents. Ethical subjects deserve to be considered in moral decisions. This group include all human beings and is increasingly seen to include non-human animals as well, especially higher mammals, and some would extend this category to plants and ecosystems. An ethical object, by contrast, is anything that is not considered ethically important in itself, such as a 5.5mm screw perhaps. These objects play a role in ethical decision-making only where they have an impact on ethical subjects.

- Within environmental ethics, four main positions can be identified. In *anthropocentrism* only humans are considered ethical subjects. *Sentientism* makes sentient animals members of the ethical community, since the ability to be a 'subject-of-a-life' or the ability to experience pain and joy is the central requirement here. In *biocentrism* all living beings are considered ethically important, since life defines the ethical community. And finally, in *ecocentrism* non-living entities such as rocky outcrops and rivers are also considered ethical subjects, or members of the ethical community, along with more systemic entities such as landscapes, ecosystems and species.

- The concept of *Nature* is not easy to define. Clearly, if it is understood as that which has not been affected by humans, there is not much of it left on the planet. However, if it is understood as that which is independent of humans and can flourish without us, more can be found. This, however, does not settle the question as to how to view entities that exist in the space between nature and culture: for example, the many animals that have been bred for millennia and plants that have been selected and "improved" for human purposes. Different ethical positions view these entities differently.

- If the ethical circle is widened beyond the realm of humans, ethical conflicts and dilemmas multiply. The likelihood that our values will come into conflict, and that ethical agents will find themselves in situations in which they cannot live up to their ethical responsibilities to humans and nature at the same time, will grow. Often taking care of nature also means taking care of humans, but not always – we cannot expect always to be in a win-win situation. One's view of nature and of the appropriate way to prioritize conflicting values depends on one's ethical viewpoint, so the clarification of these is critically important for each of us and for society as a whole.

References

Abram, David (1996): *The Spell of the Sensuous: Perception and Language in a More-Than-Human World.* New York: Vintage Books.

Bentham, Jeremy (1789)*: An Introduction to the Principles of Morals and Legislation.* http://www.econlib.org/library/Bentham/bnthPML.html

Callicott, J Baird (1980): Animal Liberation: A Triangular Affair. *Environmental Ethics* 2: 311-338.

Ferry, Luc (1992): *The New Ecological Order.* Chicago IL & London: The University of Chicago Press.

Leopold, Aldo (1949): *A Sand County Almanac.* Oxford: Oxford University Press.

Naess, Arne (1989): *Ecology, community and lifestyle: Outline of an Ecosophy* (translated and revised by David Rothenberg). Cambridge UK: Cambridge University Press.

Rawls, John (1999): *A Theory of Justice* (revised edition). Oxford: Oxford University Press.

Singer, Peter (2002): *Animal Liberation.* New York: HarperCollins.

Stone, Christopher D. (2010): *Should Trees Have Standing? Law, Morality, and the Environment* (third edition). Oxford & New York: Oxford University Press. [First published 1972]

Taylor, Paul W. (1986): *Respect for Nature: A Theory of Environmental Ethics.* Princeton NJ: Princeton University Press.

World Commission on Environment and Development (1987): *Our Common Future.* Oxford: Oxford University Press.

Further reading

Carson, Rachel (2002): *The Silent Spring 40th Anniversary Edition.* Boston MA: Houghton Mifflin Harcourt.

Krebs, Angelika (1999): *Ethics of Nature: A Map.* Berlin & New York: Walter de Gruyter.

Midgley, Mary (1983): *Animals and Why They Matter.* Athens GA: University of Georgia Press.

Norton, Bryan G. (1984): Environmental Ethics and Weak Anthropocentrism. *Environmental Ethics* 6: 131-148.

Rolston, Holmes III (1994): *Conserving Natural Value*. New York: Columbia University Press.

Warren, Mary Anne (1997): *Moral Status: Obligations to Persons and Other Living Things*. Oxford & New York: Oxford University Press.

Part II

The Right

5
Contractarianism

One way of thinking about morality is to compare it to a rule book, or a set of instructions, stating what we may and may not do. In many ways this comparison seems fair. But there are two fairly obvious problems with the idea that morality is a rulebook. The first is that we don't actually have such a rulebook, so we don't know what the rules are. The second, more important, problem is that none of us has ever "signed up" to morality. Why, then, should we live up to its rules? It might be possible to handle the signing-up problem by bringing in the idea of tacit agreement. In our day-to-day conduct all of us show our acceptance of the rules. By running our lives within ethical boundaries we tacitly agree to the application of those boundaries to all.

Is that an adequate response? Suppose I live my life within ethical boundaries most of the time, but that occasionally I cheat. Perhaps I find a gold ring and sell it, rather than handing it in to lost property. In my behaviour, am I not showing my tacit acceptance of a rulebook that permits people, occasionally, to act unethically? Isn't this the rulebook I have signed up to?

More worryingly, it can be argued that my tacit acceptance of ethical rules doesn't give me a reason to follow them. The tacit consent theorist's basic thought is that you ought to follow rules you sign up to. Ordinarily, this is true. It works perfectly well when we are dealing with the rules of a chess club. But, obviously, the thought that you ought to follow rules to which you sign up is itself an ethical principle, and so it cannot be invoked to explain why we should be moral. If I am genuinely unable to see why I should behave ethically, you won't persuade me to do so by saying that it would it would be unscrupulous, or unethical, of me not to follow rules I signed up to. My reply would be: why shouldn't I be unscrupulous?

Perhaps it is better to think of the rulebook as one anyone would sign up to if consulted. Perhaps it can also be argued that ethical rules benefit us all. This would solve both of the difficulties just mentioned. The rules can now be determined. They are the rules that we would all agree to in an imaginary world in which we are asked. And if it is asked why we would agree, the answer is simple: we would do so out of self-interest. So morality is a system of rules that each of us benefits from – and that each of us would, therefore, sign up to if asked. Of course, the devil will be in the detail, but this doesn't look like a bad idea. Moral rules are the glue that holds society together. They bind and benefit all. Although you never signed up to them, you have a powerful reason to follow these rules: doing so will ultimately benefit you. That is the idea, anyway.

Moral philosophers contrast "the Right" and "the Good". Up to this point, as the title of the first part of the book indicates, we have been examining the second of these concepts: the good. We have asked what has intrinsic, or ultimate, value. In this, the second part of the book, we want to move the discussion on and explore what philosophers refer to as "the right". Before we begin it is worth pausing to explain the distinction these rather grand-sounding terms mark. This distinction is semi-technical and doesn't follow conversational usage exactly, so a few remarks will help to put chapters 5-8 into perspective.

We often say things like "That was a good film", or "This is a good place to stop for a coffee". When we do so, we are commenting on the value of things. Obviously, the features that make a film good differ from those that make a coffee shop a good place at which to stop. Equally obviously, the fact that a film or coffee shop is good will only matter to you, if you happen to want to have a coffee or see a film.

Philosophers and theologians have always been intrigued by the idea of something that is good, and that matters, *period* – something whose value doesn't depend on whatever you happen to like doing or prefer to have. They have labelled this "the good". The question ethicists are interested in is whether there is something that is good regardless of your (possibly temporary, or eccentric) needs and wants.

Essentially, the accounts of well-being explored in chapter 2 were attempts to answer this question. Each identified something – pleasure and the absence of pain, an objective list of attainments, the satisfaction of preferences, or desires – that cannot fail to make you better off simply because it is what being better off *consists in*. Chapter 3 was an exploration into the question: "can the good be reduced to welfare?" and chapter 4 was a survey into the question "who (or even what) should we count as someone (or something) for which states of affairs can be said to matter in an ethical context?"

The term "the right" can now be explained. In ethical contexts "right" and "wrong" mark the difference between acts that are morally obligatory or permissible and acts that are morally prohibited. On the face of things, a variety of factors make conduct right or wrong. It may be right for me to do something because I promised to, or because my doing so will assist a friend. An act may be wrong because it harms another person, or injures a highly evolved animal, or because it involves lying. However, once again, philosophers and theologians have been fascinated by the thought that all morally right action has something in common – what is sometimes referred to as the "right-making property" of conduct. One such property could be that it promotes the good, for example in of happiness, and that it limits the bad, for example in terms of suffering or frustration.

However, this may give rise to difficult questions about whose good should be given priority. Should I care most about my own good, or should I care equally about the good of all ethical subjects, for instance. Here it may help to compare moral reasoning with *prudential* reasoning. When we make a prudential decision we simply ask ourselves: what course of action would be best for me? Prudential reasoning, then, is about self-interest. The relationship between what it would be right to do and my own good (since I am not thinking about anyone else's) is really pretty simple: the right act is the one that maximizes my good, or well-being. Of course, there may be tricky factual questions about how best to go about maximizing one's own good, and deeper questions about short-term versus long-term self-interest are lurking in the background, but the main idea – that the "right" thing to do when acting prudentially is to maximize one's own "good" – is hardly controversial.

In the ethical sphere the situation is rarely this simple. At least, most philosophers don't think it is. My actions are likely to affect various individuals and groups, and the world as a whole, in different ways – both positively and negatively. Often there is a conflict between my own self-interest and the interests of others. Thus, for example, after paying my everyday outgoings I may have some money left. I can either spend it on myself and go on holiday to some exotic destination, or donate some or all of it to a charity working with people living in severe poverty. The question then is: how should I handle this conflict from an ethical point of view?

In this and the next three chapters we shall examine our duties in situations of conflict, and ask what these duties are based on – or why we should do as they dictate. Thus our focus will be on the questions: Do

I have a duty not to harm or to help others, and if so how far does that duty go? Does it matter who these others are? Do I have special duties to those who are close to me, or should I prioritize the interests of those who are in most need? And what is my motivation for doing what duty requires of me?

In this chapter we confine discussion to an influential, minimalistic approach to these questions. According to this approach – the "contractarian" theory of morality – I have no duty *fundamentally* to do anything other than look after my own interests. However, this doesn't mean that ethical principles are of no interest to me. Those principles actually *serve* my interests, and any duties which run counter to my immediate interests are worth observing as well, since compliance with them will promote my interests indirectly or in the long run.

It seems, then, that the contractarian approach to ethics is not only a relatively straightforward theory which allows moral behaviour to be viewed as a form of self-interest, but also allows for a reasonably easy moral life. As the discussion develops we shall see that some people find it is too easy.

Self-interest as a foundation for ethics

Many ethical issues involve conflict between self-interest and altruism. The authors of this book, and almost certainly many of its readers, are in a position to perform more charitable deeds than they do. They choose not to do so out of convenience or self-interest. One obvious issue where this is relevant is helping poor people. At no great cost to ourselves, most of us could donate money, or larger sums of money than we already donate, to humanitarian organizations. Aid budgets, boosted in this way, could fund projects which alleviate hunger, malnutrition and disease among the almost 1 billion very poor people living on the Earth in 2012.

Why do we choose not to donate, or to donate relatively little, or to vote for politicians who prioritize domestic spending over aid budgets? One answer is: because we do not see any benefit to ourselves and those close to us.

Seen from one perspective, this answer sounds very selfish. One way of interpreting this is that we appear to be giving ourselves a special status that we are unwilling to grant other people, even though they are like us in all relevant respects. We fail to take the kind of principled stance that is characteristic of the ethical perspective. When I adopt an ethical perspective on my own conduct I am not just claiming that I *want* to act this way. Rather I am saying that I *ought* to act in this way. I can perfectly well say that I want *this* while you want *that* without fear of contradiction. An "ought" judgement, by contrast, implies that there is a general ethical principle in play – one that obliges me to treat like cases alike. On this principle there can be no special reference to a specific individual (in this case myself) or specific time and place. I must satisfy the so-called requirement of *universalizability*, which was most forcefully advanced by the British philosopher R.M. Hare (1919–2002), notably in Hare (1963), and which was also mentioned above in chapter 3.

Notice, however, that there is a way of justifying giving priority to oneself with a principle that passes the test of universalizability because it makes no reference to a specific person, place or time. The principle is that, ethically spoken, *we ought all to* prioritize our own interests and the interests of those we happen to care about. In formulating the principle in this way I am not making a non-universalizable exception for myself. I am adopting an entirely general view – a view that can be labelled *ethical egoism*.

Ethical egoism does not imply, however, that I have no reason to help anyone other than myself and those that I care about. What it *does* imply is that I should only help others if I, and those dear to me, will ultimately benefit. It may be a good idea to assist poor people if my doing so is likely to prevent, or discourage, them from doing things which harm my interests. Donating money might help to mitigate illegal immigration, piracy and terrorism, for instance.

The ethical egoist position, then, is that our ethical duties must ultimately derive from, and be based upon, self-interest. We are all required therefore to look after their own interests, and the only reason that can be given to explain why an individual ought to sacrifice her or his short-term self-interest is that it will benefit her or him in the long run.

This approach to ethics has a very long history. It was famously explored by Plato (429–347 BC) in the dialogue *Republic* (Book II), where one speaker, Glaucon, expresses the view that justice is an agreement entered into for mutual advantage (357a-359c). Through the mouthpiece of Socrates, Plato rejects Glaucon's view, arguing that justice is of more than merely prudential value. Fuller expositions of ethical egoism appeared much later. In *Leviathan* the English philosopher Thomas Hobbes (1588–1679) presents what is now a classic statement of the egoist position. In view of this, we begin by giving a brief introduction to Hobbes' ideas.

Hobbes' social contract

Hobbes´ primary aim was to understand the foundation of political authority. He asked: why should an individual obey a king or any other political authority? This question can be seen as a special case of the more general question, raised above, about why an individual should follow the dictates of morality.

There was a very real and grim background to Thomas Hobbes' reflections. He lived in England during a period of civil war, lawlessness and unrest. Monarchists and republicans were engaged in a bitter struggle. His starting point was a very pessimistic view of human nature. Man, he asserts, is a selfish creature, driven by passions such as dominance, aggression and envy. It is in the short-term interest of every person to live out these selfish passions. However, this would run counter to a willingness to obey the king or any other political authority. So, why should we be obedient?

Hobbes had little time for the idea, often wheeled out during this period, that monarchs are invested with authority by God. He rejected the "divine right of kings-theory". According to him, the only reason you can have to obey an authority which limits your opportunity to fulfil your short-term self-interests is that the obedience will serve your *long-term self-interest*. He sets up a thought experiment to show that it is indeed in an individual's interest to sacrifice his or her short-term interests for the sake of social order. In this experiment he imagines two political states in which a person can choose to live. One is the "state of nature". Here, each and every person lives according to her own selfish inclinations. The other is a "state of society", where every individual is subject to the authority and punitive regime of a strong ruler and therefore complies with laws governing the conduct of citizens.

The state of nature has the advantage that, in it, you can follow your own selfish inclinations. However, this comes at a price. Since everyone else is doing the same, the situation will turn into what Hobbes calls a *"war of all against all"*. And assuming, along with Hobbes, that people are of more or less equal strength, you have a rather poor prospect of achieving a dominant position. In fact it is much more likely that most people, including you, will end up in a very poor position: in the most quoted words of Hobbes, most people will live lives that are "solitary, poor, nasty, brutish, and short".

The state of society offers you a much better deal. Hobbes thought that the only stable society would be a form of dictatorship governed by an absolute ruler. It would be founded on a social contract whereby the ruler is granted power on condition that he guarantees a social order that affords people protection from other members of the state (a criminal justice system involving police and courts) and foreign states (military protection).

We won't analyse the details of Hobbes' political thinking here. We have presented his ideas in outline primarily to illustrate an important and recurrent line of thought in moral and political philosophy: even if we assume that people *are* motivated by narrow self-interest, and *can only be* motivated by selfishness, individuals may still have a reason to abide by moral or political rules that oblige them to consider the interests of others. In elaborating this view, Hobbes was the first to set out in detail what we now think of as the "contractarian" answer to the question why we should comply with moral and political norms.

Can it really be shown that self-interest gives us a reason to tell the truth, or keep promises? To get anywhere with this question we need to take a closer look at self-interest itself. Is it really true that we are all selfish? What exactly does self-interest involve?

Psychological egoism

A distinction is usually drawn between psychological and ethical versions of egoism. The psychological version claims that *as a matter of fact* human beings are always motivated by self-interest when they act. The ethical version claims that one *ought* to pursue one's own interests. Psychological egoism seems to be the starting point for Hobbes. However, one can question, first, whether this view is actually true, and second, whether the view, if it is true, forces us to accept the ethical egoist view that we *ought* to be motivated solely by self-interest.

Plainly, the claim that we are all egoists, and that the only thing that motivates us to act is self-interest, seems to overreach. Think, for example, about Mother Teresa (1910–1997), who spent more 45 years of her life caring for poor, sick, orphaned, and dying people in the slums of Calcutta and in other parts of the world, an effort for which she received many honours, including the Nobel peace prize in 1979. It seems odd to claim that people like Mother Teresa who devote their lives to caring for others are driven purely by self-interest.

The psychological egoist might reply that the claim being made is not that people cannot be motivated to do things for others, but that people's *ultimate motive* in deciding what to do is always self-interest: when we do something for others, it is always so that we can feel good and/or obtain other personal benefits – benefits, perhaps, which result from being seen as a person who is willing to help others.

This reply may be difficult to refute in the case of Mother Teresa. She seems to have been driven by a strong religious motivation. Her own personal salvation may well have been part of the equation, and it is also true that she received huge personal benefits in terms of personal honours and recognition. Critics have also questioned whether Mother Teresa actually managed to help the people in her care in the best way possible. However, it is possible to come up with other examples, which are much less susceptible to this kind of response. Consider the many reports of soldiers saving fellow soldiers by throwing themselves on grenades. Setting the possibility of an afterlife aside, the soldier making a sacrifice of this sort will immediately die and therefore cannot expect to feel good, or get any personal benefits, as a result of his deed.

To this the psychological egoist might reply by saying that the soldier who throws himself on a grenade still acts out of self-interest. He only performs the act because it is what he is motivated to do – and not because of some call of duty that goes against his personal inclination. In this respect, the soldier only does what is in his own personal interest. However, this reply suffers from two closely related problems.

One is that psychological egoism turns into a view that is true by definition. It now seems to be defining selfish action as action in accordance with one's own preferences. On this definition, it is hard to imagine any kind of action that isn't motivated in the way the egoist claims. Given that our preferences show themselves in the way we act, all voluntary acts are by definition selfish.

This may seem to be an advantage to the psychological egoist: if a view is true by definition, it is not possible to argue successfully against it. However, this advantage comes at a very high price, which is the second problem: the view becomes irrelevant to the discussion about egoism in the ordinary sense of the word, where not all acts need to be selfish. Let us elaborate this problem further.

Predominant egoism

We normally distinguish between people who act in a purely selfish way and people who act with varying degrees of regard for the interests of others. When the boss of a large bank, for example, expends his energy securing his own financial position rather than looking after the interests of shareholders and customers, we consider her selfish. This kind of behaviour is not uncommon. However, there are also examples of people who act in a way that most would consider unselfish.

One dramatic example was provided by Frank De Martini, an architect who worked at the Twin Towers in New York. During the attack on the World Trade Centre on 11 September 2001 he was working with his wife Nicole in the North Tower when it was hit by the first airplane. According to the *New York Times* (1 December, 2001): "When the north tower was struck, Nicole De Martini was just leaving her husband's office on the 88th floor. Finding a stairway that was still intact, he ushered her to safety. But he refused to follow just then because others needed help." De Martini went back with three helpers and was instrumental in helping more than 50 people to escape. He and his helpers all died.

It would be difficult to argue that De Martini was acting in a selfish way. Of course, all sorts of motives may have been involved. For example, before the event he gave public testimony saying that the towers would be able to withstand a collision from a modern airplane, and therefore he may have felt some personal responsibility. However, he was by all normal standards acting in an unselfish, indeed heroic, way because he risked (and lost) his own life to help others in a situation in which he could easily have chosen to escape.

Psychological egoism, in the revised version fleshed out above, then, prevents one from making useful distinctions between different kinds of behaviour – e.g. between the soldier who jumps on the grenade and the soldier who pushes his friend on to the grenade. Both have to be categorized as selfish, and equally so, from the perspective of this kind of egoism, and this is completely at odds with the way we ordinarily distinguish between selfish and unselfish acts.

Let us assume, then, as we surely have to, that it is possible for conduct to be unselfish in the ordinary sense of the word. The stubborn psychological egoist still has room for manoeuvre. For it can now be claimed that, although this kind of conduct is possible, it rarely or never occurs as a matter of fact.

The claim is no longer that all acts are by definition selfish. It is that in most, or all, cases people act in a selfish way. The American philosopher Gregory Kavka (1947–1994) once called this predominant egoism:

> *In [its] most general form, Predominant Egoism says that self-interested motives tend to take precedence over non-self-interested motives in determining human actions. That is, non-self-interested motives usually give way to self-interested motives when there is a conflict. As a result, we may say that human action in general is predominantly motivated by self-interest.* (Kavka 1986, p. 64)

Depending on how idealistic you are, this view has a certain initial plausibility. In any case, let us assume for the sake of argument that psychological egoism, now defined as predominant egoism, is true, and that therefore more often than not, though not always, human beings are motivated by self-interest. What implications does this have for what we *ought* to do? Does *ethical* egoism follow, or even gain support, from Kavka's predominant egoism?

Ethical egoism

Suppose someone says: "I am the kind of person who, at the end of the day, only cares about himself and his own interests, so therefore I should only care about myself – no reason for feelings of guilt or second thoughts." To this an obvious reply would be: "Stop being so smug and get a grip – there is no reason to turn your egoism into a virtue!"

Looking at matters from a more theoretical and less personal point of view, we can start by noting that the inference from psychological to ethical egoism is not logically valid. As argued by the Scottish philosopher David Hume (1711–1776) and his many later followers, this can be supported by appeal to the general principle that one cannot derive an "ought" (such as the ethical egoist's claim that we ought to act self-interestedly) from an "is" (a factual statement such as predominant egoist's claim that we tend to act selfishly). To obtain to an "ought" one would need at least one ethical statement among the premises from which one is arguing.

Against this, however, another principle can be set: the principle that "ought" implies "can". This reminds us, very roughly, that there is no point in saying that we ought to do something if we are not *able* to do so. Given this, it might be possible to find support for ethical egoism in predominant egoism after all. One could say that any ethical "ought" that requires us to do more than look primarily after our own self-interest is asking us to do something we cannot do and is therefore untenable. This criticism might be applicable to very strong requirements. Consider the biblical injunction, stated in the Old Testament (Leviticus 19:18) and reaffirmed by Jesus (Mark 12:31), to "love your neighbour as yourself". Can you actually do this? If you can't, is the command realistic? And if it isn't, what sense does it make to impose it? In a similar way, the ethical egoist's argument is that his position is the only tenable one: it is the only position that allows us to act in the only way we are capable of, i.e. mainly self-interestedly.

Another option is to argue that the conflict between ethical egoism and common sense ideas about our ethical obligations is not as important as it appears at first glance. Ethical egoism says we should pursue our self-interest. Arguably, on its most sensible interpretation, this injunction requires us to focus on what is in our interests *in the long run*. To fulfil this requirement we may sometimes have to forego short-term benefits to gain greater rewards later, and we may even have to abide by moral principles running counter to what at first glance seems to be our own interests. In other words, blinkered pursuit of self-interest is unlikely serve you in the long run. Respect for some additional norms, or principles, is likely to be necessary as well. A nice illustration of this is provided by the so-called "prisoner's dilemma".

The prisoner's dilemma

The prisoner's dilemma is a well-known problem in "game theory" – a form of applied mathematics that aims to model behaviour in strategic situations. The dilemma can be presented in the following way:

> *Two suspects are arrested by the police. The police have insufficient evidence for a conviction, and, having separated both prisoners, visit each of them to offer the same deal. If one testifies for the prosecution against the other and the other remains silent the betrayer goes free and the silent accomplice receives the full 10-year sentence. If both remain silent, both prisoners are sentenced to only six months in jail for a minor charge. If each betrays the other, each receives a five-year sentence. Each prisoner must choose to betray the other or to remain silent. Each one is assured that the other would not know about the betrayal before the end of the investigation. How should the prisoners act?* (Wikipedia)

Assume that the self-interested goal of both prisoners is to serve as short a time as possible in prison. Assume further that the way one prisoner acts will have no effect on the way the other prisoner acts – in particular, that there is no way for the prisoners can communicate to strike a deal with each other. Then, according to normal standards of rationality, it will be rational for each prisoner to betray the other. This can be seen in the following diagram, which outlines the possible outcomes, depending on the decisions of the two prisoners:

	Prisoner B remains silent	**Prisoner B betrays**
Prisoner A remains silent	Each serves 6 months	Prisoner A: 10 years Prisoner B: goes free
Prisoner A betrays	Prisoner A: goes free Prisoner B: 10 years	Each serves 5 years

Try to look at the situation from the point of view of prisoner A. Assume first that prisoner B remains silent. Then it will be in the self-interest of A to betray, because that will reduce his sentence from 6 months to no prison sentence at all. Assume, second, that prisoner B betrays. In this case, it will also be in the self-interest of A to betray, since this will reduce the sentence from 10 to 5 years. So whatever B does, it will be rational for A to betray B. So betrayal is what is known as the "dominant strategy" in game theory.

However, exactly the same can be said of B. Hence, if both A and B act rationally according their own self-interest the result will be that each will end up serving a 5-year prison sentence. But they could have got away with only 6 months had they both remained silent. This serves to illustrate that sometimes the best result, from a purely selfish point of view, is not achieved if everyone just does what is rationally demanded by self-interest. If both prisoners had followed a strategy based on the principle that under normal circumstances one should never betray a fellow prisoner, each would only have had to serve a 6-month sentence instead of 5 years in prison.

According to contractarian ethics this sheds light on the moral world. Ethical norms and principles can be viewed as elements of strategies we set up to get the most out of our lives. The hypothesis pursued by contractarian philosophers is that a strategy, including a number of ethical norms and principles, involving concern for others, may, in the long run, generate the best possible outcomes for us. Thus this strategy may be superior to a strategy where we pursue our own self-interest without the assistance interpersonal principles can provide. The clear advantage of this approach, for the contractarian, is that it automatically builds a very close link between ethical requirements and human motivation: it shows that self-interest and moral decency are not in conflict.

Contractarian ethics

Let us explore these ideas further. The most prominent proponent of contractarian ethics is the Canadian-American philosopher David Gauthier. In *Morals by Agreement*, published in 1986, he elaborates and defends a specifically contractarian foundation for morality and tries to argue that rationality requires one to act in accordance with moral norms.

Gauthier defines welfare in terms of preference satisfaction (see chapter 2) and takes as his starting point the assumption that we all aim to maximize our own welfare. To establish moral limits on our individual attempts to maximize our welfare, he imagines a hypothetical bargaining situation in which we all meet and try to negotiate a deal. The outcome of the deal is a set of moral norms that everyone will agree to comply with. These norms will serve as constraints on the ability of each to satisfy short-term interests. However, there will also be gains.

Two kinds of gain will be generated by the collective acceptance of moral norms. In the spirit of Hobbes there will be what one might call "negative gains": that is, others will refrain from robbing, murdering, and in other ways harming you in pursuit of their own interests. But there will also be "positive gains" in the form of the direct benefits of collaboration with others. For example, two individuals can set up a firm and, by combining their talents, achieve much more than they would have done had they acted alone.

Of course, much collaboration will take place within the framework of a capitalist market in which the guiding aim of each individual is to maximize welfare by trying to sell goods (including personal labour) at the highest possible price and to buy goods at the lowest. This is fully in the spirit of Gauthier, who claims that "markets and morals share the non-coercive reconciliation of individual interest with mutual benefit" (Gauthier 1986, p. 14). However, the market cannot stand alone – it can only function effectively within the framework of a well-functioning society, and this requires people to be, in general, honest abiders by the rules.

So, in the hypothetical bargaining situation, you, I and all other rational individuals are offered a deal whereby we trade some of our freedom to pursue our short-term interests for the gains of collective compliance with a set of moral norms. Since, according to the assumptions made by Gauthier, we are only motivated by self-interest, we will all try to maximize our gains and minimize our losses. Although there is a sense in which the outcome will be less than ideal, it will still be much better than the outcome of non-cooperation, where everyone pursues his or her short-term interests without limit.

Each person must make a bid that is good enough to convince others to strike a deal and to comply with it. Because each individual is only willing to sacrifice the minimum in order to strike a functioning deal, but no more than this, Gauthier asserts that the principle of "minimax relative concession" is sufficient to ground a number of moral principles:

> ... *many of our actual moral principles and practices are in effect applications of the requirements of minimax relative concession to particular contexts. We may suppose that promise-keeping, truth-telling, fair dealing, are to be defended by showing that adherence to them permits persons to co-operate in ways that may be expected to equalize, at least roughly, the relative benefits afforded by interaction. These are among the core practices of the morality that we may commend to each individual by showing that it commands his rational agreement.* (Gauthier 1986, p. 156)

In other words, everyone will consider it to be worth the effort to comply with certain basic moral norms as long as they trust others to do the same. The norms mentioned by Gauthier – requiring promise-keeping, truth-telling and fair dealing – seem useful from any perspective. However, what about norms governing the sharing of goods? Couldn't significant potential conflicts of interest arise among the contractors over these? Doesn't it seem unlikely that such norms will flow from the principle of minimax relative concession? These questions lead to a discussion of contractual compliance, and how to secure it.

Why comply with the contract?

Suppose I am a talented person with access to ample resources and you are a poor person with limited talents. In this case, during negotiations on a moral contract you may opt for norms that require rich people to share their possessions with poor people – a contract that I will probably oppose. How should this conflict be solved?

According to Gauthier, the answer to this question will depend on why there is this difference between the two of us. If there is no relation between you being poor and me being rich then there will be no reason to redistribute. However, if you are poor because I (or my ancestors) have taken advantage of you (or your ancestors) then, according to Gauthier, there is justification for re-distribution. The argument for this is as follows:

> *Otherwise those who consider themselves taken advantage of in initial acquisition will perceive society as unfair, in demanding payments from them without offering a compensating return, and will lack sufficient reason to accept market arrangements or to comply voluntarily with co-operative joint strategies.* (Gauthier 1986, p. 201)

Is the claim made here true? Wouldn't poor people think that a limited deal which does not involve wealth redistribution is better than no deal? Relatively speaking, they still may have more to gain than the wealthy individuals: the latter can use their wealth to identify individual solutions capable of protecting them against the negative consequences of non-cooperation. The passage just quoted suggests Gauthier would reply that the poor will still refuse to comply, because they find the arrangement "unfair".

However, this reply raises some very fundamental questions about Gauthier's contractarian project. In summary, one of the main attractions of the project is its potential to explain how people who are motivated merely by self-interest would still buy into some form of morality as a means to secure their long-term interests. Appeals to fairness aren't mentioned in this summary. It now looks as if Gauthier is smuggling in an assumption that the contractors are motivated, not only by self-interest, but by moral intuitions about what is "fair" and "reasonable".

Again, this kind of intuition seems to play a role in explaining why contractors will abide by the deals they have struck even in situations where, from their own point of view, it make better sense not to honour their contractual undertakings. Gauthier is aware of this problem:

> *The genuinely problematic element in a contractarian theory is not the introduction of the idea of morality, but the step from hypothetical agreement to actual moral constraint. Suppose that each person recognizes himself as one of the parties to agreement. The principles forming the object of agreement are those that he would have accepted ex ante in bargaining with his fellows, had he found himself among them in a context initially devoid of moral constraint. Why need he accept, ex post in his actual situation, these principles as constraining his choices? A theory of morals by agreement must answer this question.* (Gauthier 1986, p. 9)

If I am driven by self-interest, why should I remain faithful to the moral contract? Why not attempt to free-ride on the virtuous efforts of others? The prisoner's dilemma is instructive here. To put it brutally, if others are busy honouring the moral deal I can surely do rather well by cheating them, and if others are cheating me, I risk being ripped off unless I cheat as well. Non-compliance seems to be the rational strategy in both scenarios. Any sensible egoist would be a free rider.

Gauthier tries to answer this by turning the argument on its head. The only way to avoid the negative consequences of free riding is for everyone, or at least most us, to become what Gauthier calls "constrained maximizers" of self-interest. We must *internalize* the agreed moral principles, and in this way come to be disposed to act morally, rather than cheat.

Gautier's thought here is that to do what is in your best interests *in the long run* you need to be trained (by those close to you), or to train yourself (if you can), to stop thinking primarily in terms of your own self-interest and to think instead in the terms dictated by the relevant moral norms. You need to internalize moral norms so that you feel bound by them. But in the end this is a strategy of self-interest.

Critics of this solution to the problem of free riding have argued that Gauthier is smuggling in the moral point of view that the contractarian theory was supposed to ground. They don't see him providing a very good reason why someone who is solely motivated by

81

self-interest should not free ride; and they infer that it takes more than rational self-interest to motivate someone to act morally.

If the critics are right, Gautier's attempt to found morality on self-interest and rationality is doomed. However, this need not mean that the whole contractarian project has to be abandoned. We could retreat to a more modest contractarian position claiming merely that moral principles, or limits, should be minimized and based upon the mutual advantage of those who belong to the moral community. On this alternative view – "contractarianism lite" – we are morally required to consider the interests of those *with whom we can strike deals which are beneficial for both parties*, but not others. And as Gauthier acknowledges, "animals, the unborn, the congenitally handicapped and defective, fall beyond the pale of a morality tied to mutuality" (Gauthier 1986, p. 268). In the remainder of this chapter we will ask how the theory deals with one kind of being that cannot enter into a contract: animals.

Limits of moral consideration: the case of animals

Contractarian morality applies only to individuals with the capacity to enter into contracts. The American contractarian philosopher Jan Narveson has inferred from this that animals are not moral subjects and therefore have no rights:

> *On the contract view of morality, morality is a sort of agreement among rational, independent, self-interested persons, persons who have something to gain from entering into such an agreement ... A major feature of this view of morality is that it explains why we have it and who is party to it. We have it for reasons of long-term self-interest, and parties to it include all and only those who have both of the following characteristics: 1) they stand to gain by subscribing to it, at least in the long run, compared with not doing so, and 2) they are capable of entering into (and keeping) an agreement ... Given these requirements, it will be clear why animals do not have rights. For there are evident shortcomings on both scores. On the one hand, humans have nothing generally to gain by voluntarily refraining from (for instance) killing animals or 'treating them as mere means'. And on the other, animals cannot generally make agreements with us anyway, even if we wanted to have them do so ...* (Narveson 1983, pp. 56-58)

In contractarian terms, there is clearly a morally relevant difference between typical human-to-human and human-to-animal relationships. We depend on the cooperation of other people. If someone treats other another human being badly, that person will typically respond by treating him or her badly in return. By contrast, the animal community will not strike back if, for example, some of its members are used in painful experiments. From a self-interested point of view, an individual needs only to treat animals well enough for them to be fit for his or her own purposes. And in any case, as Narveson points out, non-human animals cannot enter into a contract, or agreement, governing their own and our future conduct, so they cannot enter into the moral contract which by contractarian standards serve as a criterion for being worthy of moral consideration.

The upshot, in contractarian terms, is that neither animal suffering nor the killing of animals is an ethical problem *per se*. Any form of animal use is in itself ethically acceptable. Our uses of animals may even be ethically desirable, since they usually deliver human benefits. For example, animal production is an important source of income for many people. To many more people, it is, of course, a source of convenient and delicious food. Similarly, through animal experimentation, it is possible to develop new medicines and other ways to prevent, alleviate or cure human diseases.

But the lack of moral consideration of animals does not necessarily mean the way animals are treated is irrelevant from a contractarian point of view: if people *prefer* animals to be treated in this way rather than that, for example, animal use can become an ethical issue, because it is normally in a person's interests to get what he or she prefers. However, the contractarian view of animals is resolutely anthropocentric, since any conditional "rights" to protection of this sort that the animals have will always depend on, and be secondary to, human concerns.

Most people tend to like some types of animal more than others, and they are generally more troubled by the suffering of their favourite animals. In view of this, in a contractarian society of this kind, levels of protection would differ across different species of animals. For example, if most people liked cats and dogs more than rats and seagulls, causing distress to cats and dogs would likely be viewed as a more serious problem than causing the same amount of distress to rats and seagulls.

The contractarian view accords with attitudes to animal treatment which are common across many societies. It explains why in Europe and the US, for instance, treatment of the species many people feel close to, such as cats, dogs, and horses, is usually of greater concern than our treatment of other, less popular, species. In this respect contractarianism makes our moral lives easy; we only have to think about our interactions with other adult, mentally normal, human beings. However, one may wonder whether it has become too easy.

Can it really be correct to assert that causing suffering to animals, even for an utterly trivial reason, is morally unproblematic as long as no adult, mentally normal human being is bothered by the conduct? Many people feel instinctively that it is ethically unacceptable to cause another being to suffer for little or no reason, whether one's victim is a human being or an animal. And for this reason, they may be attracted by a moral theory that attaches weight to the well-being of animals from the outset. One theory well-positioned to capture the belief that their contractual incapacity doesn't render animals ethically insignificant is "consequentialism". We shall be exploring this theory in the next chapter.

Key points

- In this chapter we have examined a theory of ethics with a historical pedigree dating back through Hobbes all the way to Plato. In this theory, the contractarian theory, the ethical arena is viewed from the self-interested perspective of the individual. The ambitious aim is to derive ethical obligations out of nothing more than self-interested cooperation.

- Often enough we find ourselves in situations where we have to ask whether we should do something which is in our own interest or something which benefits others. Those who view human nature in egoist terms will say: do what is good for *you*. This is not necessarily an ethical position. However, it becomes one if it is elevated into a universalizable principle: the principle that *all of us* ought to prioritize our own needs and interests (and perhaps the needs and interests of those close to us).

- This principle doesn't rule out your doing acts that benefit others. It is just that those acts should, in the end, benefit you in the long run. Hobbes believed that this was all we can require of human beings. As a psychological egoist, he thought that we are selfish by nature. We argued that this view cannot be stated in a way that makes it both plausible and relevant to ethics. A moderate version of it, however, predominant egoism, is defensible.

- Ethical egoism – the claim that we may and should act self-interestedly – does not follow from psychological egoism, as we saw. It was also argued that ethical egoism develops naturally from a simple-minded, and some might say rather childish, view (that you should do whatever benefits you here and now) into a more sophisticated ethical position with your long-term interests at its centre. The prisoner's dilemma was used to illustrate this. It shows that if individuals simply pursue their own self-interest in the absence of mutually beneficial agreements they end up with outcomes that are sub-optimal relative to those they would achieve if they were to cooperate, i.e. comply with norms.

- This insight is the basis of the contractarian theory of ethics developed by David Gauthier. A key subject discussed in the chapter is Gauthier's argument that allegiance to parts of normal morality may be based on a hypothetical contract whereby rational, self-interested agents agree to comply with a set of moral norms. This contract gives everyone a better deal than they would have had in a situation in which everyone just pursues their own short-term interests. Everyone has, therefore, a self-interested reason to sign up to it.

- An influential criticism of Gauthier's project is that he can only make the case convincingly if he smuggles in some form of moral norm of fairness, or reasonableness, as well as self-interest and rationality. Whatever one thinks of this criticism, contractarianism is an ethical position that distinguishes itself by the claim that morally speaking we only need to consider the interests of those on whose collaboration we depend.

- Animals do not have moral standing on the contractarianism view, but they are afforded some ethical protection when this benefits us. The chapter concluded by discussing a contractarian approach to animal ethics.

References

Gauthier, David (1986): *Morals by Agreement*. Oxford: Clarendon.

Hare, Richard M. (1963): *Freedom and Reason*. Oxford: Oxford University Press.

Kavka, Gregory (1986): *Hobbesian Moral and Political Theory*. Princeton NJ: Princeton University Press.

Narveson, Jan (1983): Animal rights revisited. In: H.B. Miller & W.H. Williams (eds.) *Ethics and animals*. Clifton NJ: Humana Press.

Plato (2004): *Republic*. Indianapolis IN: Hackett. [Written around 380 BC]

Wikipedia (undated): Prisoner's Dilemma.
http://en.wikipedia.org/wiki/Prisoner's_dilemma

Further reading

Rachels, James (2003): *The Elements of Moral Philosophy* (4th edition). New York: McGraw-Hill.

Shaver, Robert (1999): *Rational egoism: A selective and critical history*. Cambridge UK: Cambridge University Press.

Vallentyne, Peter (ed.) (1991): *Contractarianism and Rational Choice: Essays on David Gauthier's Morals by Agreement.* Cambridge UK: Cambridge University Press.

6

Consequentialism

The previous chapter presented a theory of morality based on a simple idea: that ultimately ethical behaviour should serve your interests, or maximize your welfare. The theory to be considered in the present chapter is based on a similarly simple thought: the thought that ethical behaviour serves everyone's interests, or maximizes the welfare of all. This is the guiding principle of a very popular theory of ethics known as utilitarianism. As we shall see, it is important to ask who "everyone" is, and a number of questions can also be raised about how best to "maximize" well-being. That said, obviously the suggestion that morality involves setting aside your own interests and doing whatever it takes to make the world a better place is hugely plausible. After all, what could be more important than generalized beneficence of this kind?

Historically, utilitarianism has been a prominent theory of ethics focusing on the consequences for all affected parties. Many moral philosophers today reject the classical utilitarian position, but remain committed to the consequentialist framework within which it developed. In essence, the position we wish to consider is the more general view that the ethical acceptability – the rightness or wrongness – of an act depends on whether it results in the best state of affairs possible. On this view ethical acceptability is determined by an action's outcomes, or what it does or does not achieve. The most illuminating contrast here is with theories of ethics on which certain kinds of acts, such as lying and breaking promises, are wrong, irrespective of their outcome. The consequentialist's exclusive focus on outcomes is also at odds with the familiar idea that acts done from unpleasant, or vicious, motives, such as greed or malice, are by their nature wrong. For the consequentialist, motives might tell us something about the agent's character, but they don't tell us anything about the rightness or wrongness of the act.

The Copenhagen Consensus is a think tank based in Denmark. It aims to help governments and philanthropists to identify the best way to spend aid and development funds. In 2008 it arranged an event to which a number of the world's leading economists were invited. The purpose of the meeting was to prioritize investments relating to ten different challenges that face the world, including air pollution, global warming and malnutrition.

The economists were asked the question: What would be the best way of advancing global welfare, and particularly the welfare of the developing countries? They were told that they had an additional 75 billion US dollars of resources at their disposal over a four-year initial period, and they were provided with state-of-the-art knowledge of the problems and possible solutions by leading experts in the different fields.

The economists came up with a prioritized list of 30 solutions to the different challenges. Top of the list was the provision of micronutrient supplements for children (vitamin A and zinc), which related to the challenge of malnutrition. Other solutions relating to malnutrition also came high on the list. Solutions relating to air pollution and global warming came much lower down, and none of them were on the list of 13 interventions on which money should be invested, according to the panel, given the 75 billion US dollars budget restraint.

This may seem a bit strange. The problem of malnutrition is vast and serious, but it is arguable that the problems posed by climate change, say, are much larger in scale. However, the panel looked not only at the size of the problems to be tackled, but also at the costs of solving or mitigating them. Here, interventions on malnutrition were preferred – not only because they have a significant effect, but also because they are cheap and very likely to be successful. In the words of the panel these interventions have "tremendously high benefits compared to costs". The assumption seems to have been that decisions about intervention should be guided by cost-effectiveness: the best options would be those giving the highest return in terms of problems solved per dollar spent.

Deficiency in micronutrients such as vitamin A and zinc is not only a cheap problem to solve – if it is not solved it leads to severe problems for children. Vitamin A deficiency causes an increased risk of illness and death from common infections. Alarmingly, the World Health Organization estimates that up to 250 million children suffer from it. Up to half a million of these children become blind each year. Half of them die within 12 months of losing their eyesight. Many more children suffer from a lack of mental development as a consequence of vitamin A deficiency, whilst a lack of zinc is implicated in, among other things, the susceptibility to diarrhoea from which nearly 2 million children die annually.

A great deal has already been done to prevent micronutrient deficiency in children living in the poor parts of the world, but according to the experts, there is scope to do much more at the cost of only a few dollars per child. So, although malnutrition in children is assumed to be a smaller problem than climate change, it is still, according to the Copenhagen Consensus 2008 panel, better to spend money on vitamin supplements for children than it is to spend the same amount on initiatives to prevent climate change. This is because attempting to prevent climate change will be much more expensive and the effects of the initiatives are much more uncertain.

One can, of course, discuss the factual claims from which these conclusions are drawn, and in fact many people have done so. However, it is important to see that there is also an ethical issue to be settled. The approach to prioritization applied by the Copenhagen Consensus, i.e. that we should use scarce resources so as to do maximum good, is broadly consequentialist. It is a real example of, and in some ways a test case for, the ethical perspective to be discussed in this chapter.

The consequentialist idea

According to the consequentialist it is not only true, that governments should prioritize resources in line with the logic of the Copenhagen Consensus, but that all of our resources should be used in this way. To be ethically acceptable, actions, characters, practices and policies must always generate the best possible expected total outcome. Let us try to unpack this idea.

The rather artificial sounding situation imagined by the Copenhagen Consensus, whereby an individual has to decide how to spend scarce resources so that it gives the highest possible return in terms of benefits to the people affected is, according to consequentialism, not artificial at all. Rather, this is this moral view essentially what our everyday moral life is like.

The aim of the committed consequentialist will always be to do the things that have the best possible outcome in terms of benefits for those affected, either by doing something good or preventing something bad from happening, or both. Thus, a key feature of consequentialism is its impartiality. All potential beneficiaries matter equally. It doesn't matter *who* benefits. What matters is the *total* quantity, or extent, of the benefit.

In this respect consequentialism contrasts with contractarianism. Ethical egoism, as described in the previous chapter, is partial: it says that, in deciding what to do, you may and should focus on your own gains. The consequentialist view, on the other hand, is indifferent to who receives the benefits. The only thing that matters are the total benefits, however this happens to be distributed among beneficiaries. This does not mean that your own benefit doesn't matter. The claim is just that it doesn't matter *more* than anyone else's. So consequentialism is not the same as pure altruism, according to which we should only be concerned about others. Your own good matters in within the consequentialist ethical perspective. You are required to consider all equally and not to be *selfless*.

Imagine, for example, that you are trekking in the mountains with some friends when you are suddenly caught in bad weather. You end up taking shelter in a small hut with the prospect of having to survive for up to a week in a cold place before being rescued. Before the trip, each participant agreed to bring food and water for a whole week, warm clothes and sleeping bags (just in case of an emergency). Unfortunately, half the participants have not brought these things with them, and so, through their own fault, they are stuck in the hut with nothing to eat or drink, and little to keep them warm. If you, and the other trekkers who packed the necessary supplies, don't help out, your disorganized friends will probably die before they are rescued. You can help, but by doing so you will become very hungry, thirsty and cold yourself. Should you share what you have?

According to the consequentialist you should. It does not matter that it is not your fault that others are in jeopardy. Nor does it matter that you will suffer along the way. It is no doubt true that you will suffer, but your suffering most likely won't diminish the world's supply of well-being as much as the death of your fellow trekkers, even if you suffer a great deal.

Most people would probably agree with the consequentialist here. Most of us look at the world in consequentialist terms in cases like the one described. However, to be a full-blown consequentialist we need to agree that all moral situations are in principle like the trekking example. This may be asking too much of us, as we shall see later in this chapter. However, before we discuss this claim in more detail, let us try to define consequentialism a little more precisely.

Utilitarianism

We need to start with what moral philosophers call "the good". An understanding of this term will enable us to see exactly how consequentialism differs from other ethical theories on offer. It will also explain why it is often said that consequentialism "defines the right in terms of the good".

Philosophers use "the good" to refer to whatever is valuable in its own right. Questions about what *is* good in its own right were discussed in the first part of this book (chapters 2-4). We discovered that at various times it has been held that mental states, satisfied preferences, and objectively listed items such as friendship and knowledge are the only intrinsically valuable things. We also saw that questions about the good are generally treated as questions about what constitutes well-being, or welfare. The point here, however, is this: the consequentialist asserts that, quite generally, the *right thing to do is always to maximize the good*. In other words, ethically speaking, *we should always do whatever will produce the most of what is valuable in itself.*

It can be seen at once that consequentialism can be fleshed out in variety of ways, depending on the theory of the good it incorporates. A form of consequentialism based upon a hedonist account of the good will differ from one based upon preference-satisfaction. Utilitarianism, as we noted above, has been the predominant form of consequentialism. In its classical form, it is the view that morally right action brings about the greatest possible amount of happiness, with happiness being understood in terms of a balance of pleasure over pain. The founding father of what we now think of as utilitarianism is Jeremy Bentham. In chapter 2 we saw that Bentham was a hedonist. He thought pleasure is the only thing that matters, or is valuable, in its own right. Pain is an intrinsic disvalue. In the following passage Bentham explains what he calls the *principle of utility*:

> *By the principle of utility is meant that principle which approves or disapproves of every action whatsoever, according to the tendency it appears to have to augment or diminish the happiness of the party whose interest is in question: or, what is the same thing in other words, to promote or to oppose that happiness. I say of every action whatsoever, and therefore not only of every action of a private individual, but of every measure of government.* (Bentham 1789, Chapter 1)

According to Bentham, then, each of us should aim to create happiness. Equally, the policies adopted by political institutions are to be assessed by their tendency to bring about, or to thwart, the happiness of citizens. Bentham himself devoted a great deal of time to criticize and improve the criminal code. He was trained as a lawyer, and he considered the penal system in England in the late eighteenth century irrational and immoral. Utilitarian thinking has actually had quite a profound effect on this area.

Punishment uses various devices – fines, imprisonment, sometimes capital punishment – to damage the interests of those who break the law. The utilitarian worry about this, as Bentham saw, is that it just adds more misery to misery. First, harm is caused by a crime. Then, more harm is done, this time punitively. The punishment of criminals appears, therefore, to be at odds with the principle of utility, since that principle bids us to act always in a way that increases the welfare of all, including criminal offenders.

The utilitarian position is that punishment can only be justified if it prevents more harm than it creates. This may happen directly, when a criminal is held in jail and thereby prevented from committing more crimes, or indirectly, either by reforming the character of the criminal or by deterring potential criminals from engaging in criminal activities. The view that punishment is, on balance and over the long term, beneficial to society and adds to human welfare is accepted by most of those who work professionally in the criminal justice system. Many people would see this as the reason why we punish offenders. However, it is also clear from public controversies about the punishment of criminals who have been violent to wholly innocent victims or abused small children, for example, that others do not share this view. Substantial numbers of people regard punishment as a form of retribution: we are entitled to lock up criminals, not because this will bring about a welcome outcome, though it might, but because they deserve it.

In some places Bentham claims that according to utilitarianism "*the greatest happiness of the greatest number*" is the measure of right and wrong. This is a nice slogan, but it contains a serious ambiguity. It speaks both about the greatest sum of happiness and the greatest number of people affected. Very often these two dimensions of value will be in harmony, since sharing resources between many needy people rather than awarding them to a few individuals will usually result in the highest level of total welfare. However, it is not difficult to come up with examples where this is not the case.

During wars and following disasters such as earthquakes, doctors and paramedics are sometimes forced to make difficult choices about who to help. They may be short of skilled personnel, or lack medicine or equipment. If the aim is to do the maximum good in terms of the number of people who survive, the best policy for the doctors may be, not to help as many as possible, but rather to focus on a smaller group of those who are most likely to survive if treated. This is a tough decision for doctors to make. But in situations of this kind it is normal to try to secure the greater good in terms of the number of people surviving, rather than simply trying to help as many people as possible. This is exactly what is recommended from the utilitarian perspective. The slogan of utilitarianism should only be "the greatest happiness", while the slogan of consequentialism should be "the greatest good."

As we saw in chapter 2, simple hedonism is not the only account of what is meant by welfare. Bentham's heir and fellow utilitarian, John Stuart Mill, argued for a modified hedonistic position that attached greater value to higher pleasures (e.g. music and poetry) than it does to lower ones (e.g. food or visits to the sauna). He did so to fend off the accusation that his view "that life has ... no higher end than pleasure" is a "doctrine worthy only of swine." Reassuring his readers that we are better off as discontented human beings than we would be as cheerful pigs, Mill presented a form of utilitarianism in which higher pleasures are much more likely than lower pleasures to be promoted by morality. Modern utilitarians, such as Peter Singer, are more likely to defend utilitarian positions in which the thing to be maximized – sometimes called the *maximand* – is preference satisfaction. Accordingly, their view is sometimes labelled "preference utilitarianism". For Singer, then, morally right action is action that results in the highest level of preference satisfaction, net of preference frustration.

So what all utilitarian theories of ethics have in common is this: they define right action as action maximizing utility, and they equate utility with welfare. The main difference between the various forms of utilitarianism lies in the way welfare is understood. In the classical accounts of the late eighteenth century and early nineteenth century it was taken to be happiness, which was in turn defined in terms of pleasure and the absence of pain. Mill introduced a distinction between higher and lower pleasures. Later writers have worked with preference satisfaction.

The terms "utility", "the good" and "welfare" are very often used interchangeably in discussions of consequentialism. However, the consequentialist outlook can be combined with the idea that things other than welfare are intrinsically valuable, or good. The British philosopher G. E. Moore (1873–1958) took this path. He defended a non-welfarist form of consequentialism in which the goal remains that of promoting the good, but in which goodness is a property belonging to things other than human welfare. This is sometimes called "ideal utilitarianism". Moore declared that the most valuable states we know of are the pleasures of friendship and aesthetic enjoyment.

Consequentialism: an agent-neutral perspective

The consequentialist approach may be assessed by looking at its application in situations where it is agreed that it would be valuable to promote or prevent a certain kind of consequence – for example, to prevent innocent people with good lives ahead of them from being killed. In situations like this consequentialists focus solely on achieving the best outcome. They believe that the right thing to do is to maximize positive, and minimize negative, outcomes. Their non-consequentialist critics, unconvinced by this focus, insist that it is necessary to take into consideration things other than outcomes. The following example, provided by the British philosopher Bernard Williams (1929–2003), is illustrative here:

> *Jim finds himself in the central square of a small South American town. Tied up against the wall are a row of twenty Indians, most terrified, a few defiant, in front of them several armed men in uniform. A heavy man in a sweat-stained khaki shirt turns out to be the captain in charge and, after a good deal of questioning of Jim which establishes that he got there by accident while on a botanical expedition, explains that the Indians are a random group of the inhabitants who, after recent acts of protest against the government, are just about to be killed to remind other possible protestors of the advantages of not protesting. However, since Jim is an honoured visitor from another land, the captain is happy to offer him a guest's privilege of killing one of the Indians himself. If Jim accepts, then as a special mark of the occasion, the other Indians will be let off. Of course, if Jim refuses, then there is no special occasion, and Pedro here will do what he was about to do when Jim arrived, and kill them all. Jim, with some desperate recollection of schoolboy action, wonders whether if he got hold of a gun, he could hold the captain Pedro and the rest of the soldiers to threat, but it is quite clear from the set-up that nothing of that kind is going to work: any attempt at that sort of thing will mean that all the Indians will be killed, and himself. The men against the wall, and the other villagers, understand the situation, and are obviously begging him to accept. What should he do?* (Smart & Williams 1973, pp. 98-99)

Of course, there is bound to be uncertainty about what will actually happen when Jim does, or does not, shoot the Indian. Putting this uncertainty and any legal issues aside, however, it is quite clear what should be done from a consequentialist perspective: Jim should *of course* shoot the one Indian. If he does, one person will die, but nineteen will survive. If he does not, the one Indian will still be killed, but along with all his comrades. Jim will feel guilty for the rest of his life if he kills an innocent person, but he is likely to feel at least as guilty if, by refusing to kill the Indian, he ends up feeling responsible for nineteen unnecessary deaths. Thus from a consequentialist perspective the correct decision is obvious: Jim should kill the Indian.

Bernard Williams tends to agree with this conclusion. However, he strongly disagrees that the conclusion is obvious. He argues that there are similar situations in which the contrast between the possible outcomes is less stark, and where the right decision may be to do what brings about a suboptimal outcome. The alternative, non-consequentialist view emerging seems to be that what matters, from a moral point of view, is not only the *consequences* of what we do, but what we *do* in itself. If Jim does not shoot one Indian, then twenty Indians will be shot, but *he* personally will not shoot any of them.

As we shall see later in this book, some philosophers believe that there is a moral difference between doing something and causing something to happen as a consequence of not doing something, as in Jim's case. This is an example of what is called an "agent-relative" morality: here the position of the agent makes a difference to what it is morally right to do. It is Pedro's choice to kill the Indians. Why should Jim let himself get caught up into Pedro's murderous schemes? Jim is not responsible for what Pedro does. Something like this, at any rate, might be argued by a non-consequentialist in this case.

The ethical egoism discussed in the previous chapter is a different kind of agent-relative moral view. Here, it matters morally whether the consequences befall the agent or someone else – and the preferred act is always the one which benefits the agent the most. As we shall see, other agent-relative positions hold that what matters is whether an outcome is intentionally caused by the actions of the agent or by someone else.

Suppose we alter the example of Jim and the Indians slightly. Now Jim has the choice to either kill one of the Indians, or let another person kill the Indian and beat another very badly. Legal issues aside, many people would say that *of course* Jim should *not* kill the Indian. Not because of the way the consequences add up, but because killing someone is an extreme act that one should do only in the most exceptional situations. For the consequentialist, on the other hand, whether or not Jim should kill the Indian in this situation depends on how the consequences add up. They may very well add up in such a way that Jim should not kill the Indian – for example, because the harm he will suffer by killing the Indian will be more than that experienced by the Indian who is going to be beaten up if he refrains from doing so. In the consequentialist perspective, then, the conclusion that Jim should refuse to kill the Indian cannot be taken for granted. It all depends on how the consequences add up.

An important point to notice here is that, as far as a consequentialist is concerned, judgments about the right action to take are impersonal: whether the situation is seen from the point of view of the agent, in this case Jim, or a third party is irrelevant. In this respect consequentialism is an agent-*neutral* ethical theory, rather than an agent relative one. The morally preferred line of action does not depend on whether you see the situation from the point of view of the acting person, or from the point of view of a benevolent spectator, for example. In principle, there is no difference between the way the moral agent should see his or her situation and the way an ideal independent observer would view the same situation.

Does the end always justify the means?

In the case described above, it was assumed that there are powerful ethical objections to the killing of innocent people. We also contemplated the idea that it may be morally right to kill an innocent person if it is the only way to prevent someone from doing something much worse. In a familiar phrase, the *end* (preventing innocent people from being killed) justifies the *means* (killing an innocent person). In the case of Jim, as described by Bernard Williams, it might be considered that there are mitigating circumstances if the Indian Jim is considering killing is begging to be killed.

However, there are bound to be other cases in which no such mitigating circumstances can be identified, and in these cases the consequentialist view, which allows the end to justify the means, becomes problematic. One case of this sort has been presented by the Australian philosopher H. J. McCloskey (1969, pp. 180-181). He asks us to imagine a sheriff in a town in the southern part of the USA, perhaps sometimes in the 1960s, who is faced with a difficult dilemma:

A white girl has been raped. In the local community, it is widely believed that a certain black man is guilty of committing the crime. However, the sheriff knows that the man is innocent. But, he also knows that if he does not press charges against the man, riots against black people will probably break out and these riots, given the very tense situation, will probably end in a loss of life. What would we want the sheriff to do in this fictional, but not entirely unrealistic, case?

It appears that, from a consequentialist point of view, the sheriff should frame the black man, thus ensuring that he is sent to prison, and perhaps even executed, for a crime of which he is not guilty. Obviously, however, this is completely at odds with our beliefs about justice and fairness. The case therefore seems to show that utilitarianism, and consequentialism more generally, are flawed ethical theories. The problem, as McCloskey sees it, is that utilitarianism allows the end to justify unjust means.

There are roughly two ways in which the consequentialist can respond to this kind of case. The *first* is to point to indirect negative consequences which may follow if those who are responsible for enforcing the law, like the sheriff, ignore it for the sake of expediency. Public trust in the criminal justice system is an important factor in the smooth functioning of modern society. In the case we are considering, for example, it can be anticipated that riots might well occur if it were discovered that the sheriff has framed a young black man to appease a white mob. So there are very good consequentialist reasons why those who are responsible for upholding the law should act with integrity and not allow exceptions based on short-sighted consequentialist calculations.

Critics of consequentialism can reasonably point out that this response will not always be available. Thus the circumstances might be such that the miscarriage of justice would never be discovered. The sheriff may be a person of high moral standards who decides to deviate from his law-abiding principles only in this very exceptional case. What happens then? At this point the consequentialist needs to offer a *second* line of response. The argument has to be that exceptional cases call for exceptional responses, and that it is actually an advantage of consequentialism that it allows for this. In any case, in real-life cases of this troubling sort, consequentialist decisions are sometimes made.

This may sound outrageous, or even corrupt. However, history does indeed provide examples of consequentialist decisions and policy-making. In Denmark after the Second World War and the German occupation, for example, there was a judicial purge. A number of people were convicted for collaborating with the German occupational forces during the war. Such collaboration was not illegal during the war, so the convictions had to be based on retrospective laws – a practice flouting the usual norms of criminal justice. This strategy seems to have been accepted by those in positions of authority in order to avert greater social ills. There was an extremely tense situation just after the war, of course. There was a real possibility that people would take the law into their own hands, which would have resulted in much worse consequences, as happened in some other European countries. Later, when things had calmed down, a lot of cases were dropped.

Levels of moral thinking

The discussion of the previous section raises a more general problem, namely: how should the consequentialist view the pre-theoretical moral norms, or rules, that we all take for granted and apply day-to-day? Where these norms clash with consequentialist guidance, are they to be given up and replaced by the principle of maximizing good consequences? What is the relationship between consequentialism as an ethical theory and common-sense morality?

Consider some ordinary precepts of morally acceptable behaviour: keep your promises, don't steal, don't attack the innocent, and so on. Such norms play an important role in human life. They help to create some order in our lives. They make social life reasonably predictable. They also simplify deliberation about how to act – basically they narrow the options.

Now suppose you are a consequentialist. You are not equipped with the precepts above. As a result you have to engage in some very demanding thought when you deliberate about what to do. Nor is there any respite from this: as a consequentialist you face questions about the best thing to do from the moment you open your eyes in the morning and unremittingly throughout the day.

To begin with, you have to outline all the alternative courses of action which are open to you during the day. This alone is a massive task. Instead of doing what you normally do – for example, going to work or university – you must first consider the myriad courses of action open to you. You could visit someone. You could stay home and write a letter to a newspaper. You could volunteer to work for a humanitarian organization. You could … And so on. It is obvious you have a huge number of options to consider.

Going into a little more detail, for each course of action you must identify and estimate all the consequences: you must calculate the impact of each option on the welfare of all affected parties for now *and* the future. You must then calculate the total expected welfare for each course of action in order to be able to decide which action gives the largest total sum of welfare. On top of this, you will, perhaps, be obliged to consider how doing one thing in the morning will affect your ability to do another thing in the afternoon.

This whole exercise is not only complicated, time-consuming and fraught with uncertainty – it is impossible: thorough-going consequentialism, applied to practical deliberation, is quite simply self-defeating. The consequentialist therefore has a good *consequentialist reason* not to think in consequentialist terms all the time. Rather, it appears to be a better strategy to deliberate in terms of simple common sense moral precepts most of the time, or possibly an adjusted subset of these precepts that brings about the best expected overall consequences. Paradoxically, the consequentialist ideal is best served when it is at least partly ignored.

Bentham and Mill recognized that we need "rules of thumb" to be able, in practice, to apply the principle of utility, and later discussions have put even more emphasis on the role of rules. Indeed some contemporary utilitarians defend what they call "rule-utilitarianism". In this theory the role of consequentialist thinking is not to assess individual acts, but rather to assess enduring rules of conduct. Hence, the principle of utility for these later writers is not "Do whatever maximizes welfare in the present situation" but "Abide by rules whose observance by all would maximize welfare".

Rule-utilitarianism has been widely criticized for two main reasons. First, it has proved hard to specify rules that qualify as maximizing. Life is simply too complex. But second, why should we follow the rules that would give the best outcome if all comply, when we know that a significant number of people won't do the same? The notion that we should abide by rules even when we know others aren't doing so, and even when secretly breaking the rules would be more beneficial, has been disparaged by the more traditional act-utilitarians as "rule worship". Such worship, it is said, is hardly in the spirit of consequentialism.

Today, rule-utilitarianism is a minority view, albeit it has some quite prominent supporters. In any event, the idea that, as a consequentialist, one often needs some simple, pragmatic rules, or guides to conduct, is very much alive. According to an influential articulation of this idea, we need two levels of moral thinking. At the everyday, *intuitive* level, we use conventional moral precepts as our guide. However, sometimes, in a quiet moment of reflection perhaps, we step back from ordinary moral practice and switch to a *critical* level of moral thinking at which we assess and adjust the everyday precepts. In this picture the consequentialist principle serves as a moderator of common-sense ethical thought – a criterion against which we can assess and adjust the moral norms and strategies that normally guide our actions.

Animal ethics: reform or radical change?

To continue the animal ethics theme from previous chapters: What attitudes do consequentialists have to animal ethics? The use of animals in the production of food and other human consumables such as leather is an integral part of western culture. Until quite recently, most viewed this use as a necessity, or at any rate not a matter for moral debate. However, since at least the 1960s our awareness of the negative effects of intensive farming on animal welfare has grown. Animal welfare worries an increasing number of people. Calves in veal crates, hens in small battery cages, and tethered or stalled sows, are some of the better-known practices causing public concern. What is the consequentialist to make of this?

The utilitarian Peter Singer has argued powerfully and vociferously since the 1970s that the interests of animals are on a par with human interests.

> I am urging that we extend to other species the basic principle of equality that most of us recognize should be extended to all members of our own species. ... Jeremy Bentham incorporated the essential basis of moral equality into his utilitarian system of ethics in the formula: "Each to count for one and none for more than one." In other words, the interests of every being affected by an action are to be taken into account and given the same weight as the like interests of any other being. A later utilitarian, Henry Sidgwick, put the point in this way: "The good of any one individual is of no more importance, from the point of view (if I may say so) of the Universe, than the good of any other." ... The racist violates the principle of equality by giving greater weight to the interests of members of his own race, when there is a clash between their interests and the interests of those of another race. Similarly the speciesist allows the interests of his own species to override the greater interests of members of other species. The pattern is the same in each case. (Singer 1989, pp. 152-153)

For utilitarians like Singer what matters ethically is simple yet radical in its implications: it is the interests of anyone, or any living being, affected by what we do, including all sentient creatures. In particular, the *species* of beings affected by what we do is irrelevant. The way we treat animals currently, Singer argues, is objectionable in the same way as racism. Indefensibly, it attaches moral significance to a difference between "us and them" that makes no difference. It is a clear case of "speciesism".

This view has serious implications for modern animal production. In intensive farming the basic interests of animals are often set aside so that production can be efficient, and to allow consumers to buy cheap meat and other animal products. But in affluent regions of the world, at least, access to inexpensive food is not actually *needed*. Indeed most people in the west could manage without any meat or other animal products at all. With suitable adjustments to diet and lifestyle, their current level of welfare could be maintained. They might even enjoy greater welfare in the long run, in virtue of their better health and extended longevity. At any rate, Singer's argument is quite straightforward: we should all stop eating meat and other animal products. This would solve the welfare problem in animal production, since if we all cease to consume animal products there will be no farm animals around to suffer. However, there are two obvious problems with this approach.

First, as is now being demonstrated increasingly in the organic sector, there is an alternative approach on offer. Farm animals can be provided with better lives and, at the same time, most humans in the rich parts of the world at least can enjoy affordable animal products (assuming that the price of organic products will fall when organic production or other forms of alternative production become more wide-spread). Livestock welfare can be maintained at what is arguably a level where the lives of the animals are worth living Is this not better from a utilitarian point of view? Of course, animals would still have to be slaughtered, but this need not be a problem for the utilitarian as long as the animals are killed in a painless way and are replaced by other animals which live equally good lives. Singer agrees with this point in principle, but he argues that in practice this is not how things will work out. He asserts that if we don't stop eating meat, animal production will continue to be more or less the same, unaffected by concerns about animal welfare. He clearly doesn't believe that welfare friendly animal production will ever prevail.

This leads to the second problem. Despite approximately 50 years of debate about the way farm animals are treated, only a very small fraction of people in the West have become vegetarians. Meanwhile popular consumption of meat has steadily increased internationally with rising levels of prosperity. Against Singer, this suggests that the consequentialist needs to adopt a more pragmatic and piecemeal approach to changing people's behaviour.

Consequentialists who want to improve conditions for farm animals could, for example, pursue the strategy of improving *animal welfare*. Instead of insisting that we all become moral vegetarians, this approach looks for ways to reform animal production. This can be achieved, to some extent, by means of revised animal welfare legislation. Thus, in Europe during the last four decades, laws have been passed, first in individual countries, and later at the EU level, to outlaw methods of animal production that are perceived as cruel – for example, the confinement of veal calves in crates without access to straw and the once common use of battery hens. Also, minimum requirements for space and other resources such as the provision of straw have been established at law.

Highly motivated consumers can, of course, be encouraged to seek out, and buy, specially labelled animal products that have been produced in a welfare friendly manner. If large numbers of consumers buy products of this kind, a knock-on effect on the manner in which other animals are treated is likely. This approach has been reasonably successful in some areas. In Denmark for example, between 30-40% of eggs and milk consumed in 2010 came from alternative production systems.

The general point we are trying to get across is that there is a world of difference between the theoretical conclusions we reach in the study and the practical and policy implications of these conclusions in the messy arena of politics and commerce. In particular, in the real world, even committed consequentialists who are very clear about their goal – in the present case, an end to methods of animal production in which animals suffer needlessly – will have to give careful consideration to *strategy*, and here a good dose of pragmatism is necessary. A key issue is gradualism. Is a radical shift in practice or a gradual reform the best course? Which would be more likely to succeed, especially given that most people do not share Singer's unconditional anti-speciesism, and given indeed that most people do not look at ethical problems as consequentialists?

Obviously, these are difficult questions. It would be much easier if all individuals were convinced consequentialists – or would it?

Too demanding?

The consequentialist principle that you should act always so as to maximize the good certainly appears to be attractive. It seems to enjoin us simply to do as much good as we can in the world, which is hardly a controversial-looking ethical injunction. The principle, however, contains the word "always". Quite literally, it says that you are always obliged to do whatever is in your power to bring about good outcomes (and prevent bad ones). It doesn't matter who benefits. It may be your mother. It may be a burglar who has injured himself climbing through your window. It could be someone trying to raise funds for a cultural project in Canada, and if all sentient creatures are in the moral circle it could be a seagull.

This means that whenever you use your time or spend money you should do so in a way that generates the largest returns in terms of doing good or preventing bad. Given the problem with which this chapter began – the plight of the hundreds of millions of people who go hungry to bed every day – this has dramatic implications.

In a well-known paper Singer (1972) argued that most people in affluent countries should change their way of life radically. They should focus on helping poor people rather than trying to obtain things that are surplus to their needs. Singer's argument invoked the following innocuous-sounding principle: "if it is in our power to prevent something bad from happening, without thereby sacrificing anything of comparable moral importance, we ought, morally, to do it". Singer calls this the "minimal principle".

The minimal principle is less demanding than most forms of consequentialism, since it requires the prevention of the bad, not the promotion of the good. Nevertheless, it can still be quite demanding. For example, if you can find an international charity that will channel your savings into aid programmes working with starving families, you should do this before you do most of the things you and your family presently take for granted.

Are others also obliged to help? Of course, Singer asserts they are. However, importantly, he does not consider the fact that many will *not* help a valid excuse for not helping. He argues:

> *... if I am walking past a shallow pond and see a child drowning in it, I ought to wade in and pull the child out. This will mean getting my clothes muddy, but this is insignificant, while the death of the child would presumably be a very bad thing. ... the fact that there are millions of other people in the same position, [as regards the opportunity to help starving people], as I am, does not make the situation significantly different from a situation in which I am the only person who can prevent something very bad from occurring. Again, of course, I admit that there is a psychological difference between the cases; one feels less guilty about doing nothing if one can point to others, similarly placed, who have also done nothing. Yet this can make no real difference to our moral obligations. Should I consider that I am less obliged to pull the drowning child out of the pond if on looking around I see other people, no further away than I am, who have also noticed the child but are doing nothing?* (Singer 1972, pp. 231-233)

It can be seen, then, that consequentialism is bound to have a profound effect on the lives of those who try to live in accordance with it. In order to comply with it, you would have to organize your life so as to generate income to be passed on to starving people or others in similarly bad situations. Of the income you generate, you are entitled to retain only what you need to prevent you and your family from starving or descending into some other form of misery, and to ensure that you are able to continue to work and provide money for the poor. Ultimately, of course, your family are not to be treated by you as more important than anyone else.

But what kind of life is that? It would probably be a difficult philosophy to sell to anyone – apart from the odd individual who aspires to saintly canonization. Not even Singer himself has been able to live up to his own prescription, though he does donate a substantial amount of his salary to charities.

Consequentialism is in real trouble if the demands it makes on people are so high that they give up. Devoted consequentialists like Singer take this to show, of consequentialism, not that it should be abandoned, but rather that it should promoted with sensitivity and realism. Thus, in a recent book about how to help the poor, *The Life You Can Save* (2009), Singer describes some achievable goals. For example, we should give up certain luxuries such as bottled water and instead give what is thereby saved to effective charities. But before we infer, perhaps cynically, that he is dropping his principles, we should note that Singer's reason for lowering the level of ambition is *itself* consequentialist: by focusing realistically on what can be done, he thinks that he can motivate more charitable behaviour than he would if he were to set the bar too high.

That said, some consequentialists have recently come to the conclusion that the standard form consequentialism presented above is indeed too demanding. To use a term first introduced by the American philosopher Samuel Scheffler, they have argued that consequentialism needs to allow for an "agent-centred prerogative", permitting us to apply consequentialist thinking only after we have addressed the needs and well-being of ourselves and those dear to us. This view deals more or less satisfactorily with the issue of consequentialism being too demanding (depending on how much we are allowed to keep for ourselves).

However, to some this halfway-house – an expedient blend of consequentialism and licensed moral parochialism – will come across as little more than an arbitrary, *ad hoc* solution. They will no doubt want to look for a new theoretical starting point, as we shall also do in the next chapter.

Key points

- The aim of this chapter was to describe and discuss the consequentialist principle that we should always aim to bring about the best outcome. The key feature here is impartiality: *who* benefits is of no importance, since all that matters is the total size of the benefit.

- Consequentialism requires a definition of the good, or the thing to be maximized. Utilitarianism is the specific variety of consequentialism in which the good is defined in terms of welfare. There are different forms of utilitarianism, depending on one's definition of welfare.

- An important feature of consequentialism is that it adopts an agent-neutral perspective to our actions. It says that, in principle, there is no moral difference between, say, my killing someone or my not preventing someone else from killing the same person.

- Another feature of consequentialism that has attracted attention is that it always allows the end to justify the means – even where the means are very obviously unjust. The consequentialist can defuse alarm at this feature, to some degree, by pointing to the positive indirect consequences of upholding norms of justice.

- Living in accordance with the consequentialist principle would be very onerous. Nor would it be very productive in consequentialist terms. Hence, consequentialists tend to agree that in normal circumstances we should act in accordance with conventional moral precepts. Consequentialism is, however, still very important, as it enables us to critically assess and adjust these precepts.

- Debates often arise over the most effective moral strategy from a consequentialist perspective, and they are bound to do so, given that most people do not share the consequentialist view. Here, one can either be radical, and argue for dramatic changes to our way of life, or adopt a more pragmatic stance, allowing piecemeal reform.

- Finally, we discussed the allegation that consequentialism makes demands we could never fulfil. It was conceded that this allegation gives us a further reason to adopt a piecemeal approach to moral progress.

References

Bentham, Jeremy (1789): *An Introduction to the Principles of Morals and Legislation.* http://www.econlib.org/library/Bentham/bnthPML.html

McCloskey, H.J. (1969): *Meta-Ethics and Normative Ethics.* The Hague: Martinus Nijhoff.

Singer, Peter (1972): Famine, Affluence, and Morality. *Philosophy and Public Affairs* 1 (3): 229-243.

Singer, Peter (1989): All Animals are Equal. In: Tom Regan & Peter Singer (eds.) *Animal Rights and Human Obligations*, pp. 148-162. Englewood Cliffs NJ: Prentice Hall.

Singer, Peter (2009): *The Life You Can Save.* New York: Random House.

Smart, J.J.C. & Williams, Bernard (1973): *Utilitarianism: For and against.* Cambridge UK: Cambridge University Press.

Further reading

Driver, Julia (2006): *Ethics: The Fundamentals.* Oxford: Wiley-Blackwell.

Scheffler, Samuel (1988): *Consequentialism and its Critics.* Oxford: Oxford University Press.

7
Ethics of Rights

In 1967 the British philosopher Philippa Foot (1920–2010) published what was to become a celebrated paper on the ethics of abortion. In the paper Foot presented some brilliant "thought experiments" to test our moral intuitions. In philosophical circles and beyond, these experiments have been repeated, altered, and argued over, ever since. Foot's main interest was in aspects of our moral thinking that seem to take us outside the consequentialist perspective. Here is a scenario that has occupied several philosophers, among them the American Shelly Kagan:

> *Imagine that there are five patients, each of whom will soon die unless they receive an appropriate transplanted organ: one needs a heart, two need kidneys, one needs a liver, and the fifth needs new lungs. Unfortunately, due to tissue incompatibilities, none of the five can act as donor for the others. But here is Chuck, who is in the hospital for some fairly routine tests. The hospital computer reveals that his tissue is completely compatible with the five patients. You are a surgeon, and it now occurs to you that you could chop up Chuck and use his organs to save the five others. What should you do? ... Your choices are these: do nothing, in which case five people will die and one person will live; or chop up Chuck, in which case Chuck will obviously die but five people will live. From the utilitarian standpoint the results certainly seem to be better if you chop up Chuck. After all, if everyone counts equally, then it is simply a matter of five versus one. Obviously, it is a horrible result that Chuck will end up dead; but it would be an even worse result if five people end up dead. So the right thing to do – according to utilitarianism – is to kill Chuck. (Kagan 1998, p. 71)*

That conclusion is troubling, isn't it? Surely any moral theory that requires, or even permits, us to kill Chuck is deeply flawed. Some might go so far as to say that it is part of the purpose of morality to rule out cold-blooded 'cost-benefit analysis of this sort. But how is that to be achieved? The obvious answer is that people have rights, including the right not be killed in a grotesque organ harvest. In an ethical theory rights must be given due emphasis. Otherwise we can't explain why we shouldn't chop up Chuck.

We now turn from consequentialism to the rights-based approach to ethics. As we have seen, consequentialism takes many forms, but it has at least one defining feature: what makes an act right or wrong depends entirely on its consequences – on its propensity to promote the good – and nothing else. The consequentialist places no *constraints* on the promotion of the good. So far as the utilitarian is concerned, for example, if an action maximizes welfare it is the morally correct thing to do. This appears to clash with the very widespread conviction that we possess *rights*. A right is, precisely, a moral constraint. It "trumps" other considerations in ethical reasoning. If other people ignore your rights, they are morally wrong – not prima facie wrong, or wrong, other things being equal, but wrong *period*. Others have a moral (and not merely a legal) *duty* to respect your rights.

Let us return to the hospital and Chuck. The consequentialist approach to this case looks seriously wrong-headed. A surgeon cannot legitimately use Chuck in the way envisaged. Why, though? This turns out to be a less simple question than we first think, but few would hesitate before saying that Chuck's rights here, and specifically his very fundamental right to live, would be violated by the proposed surgery. The consequentialist simply overlooks the ethics of rights.

The "ethics of rights" is in fact a rather diverse collection of ethical positions taken up by various writers historically – it is perhaps better described as the "ethics of rights *tradition*". Writings in this tradition have one defining feature: they insist that there are ways of promoting the good as the consequentialist demands that are *morally impermissible*, or prohibited. Another way to put this is to say that they impose *constraints* on the promotion of the good. The surgeon can promote the good – i.e. collective welfare – by chopping up Chuck, but a constraint on this in the form of a right to life prohibits him from doing so.

Unsurprisingly, defenders of consequentialism are unlikely to concede that their theory *entails* that Chuck should be chopped up. They will point to various potentially catastrophic outcomes of a policy of organ "sharing". The public would become wary of visiting hospitals for fear of being harvested themselves. The needy, on the other hand, would have a strong incentive to contact hospitals with details of vulnerable people with vital organs they are really not making the most of. "My son is 21 and in the middle of a degree in Supply Chain Management! Could you not use his uncle's liver? He's depressed ... and he has gout!" But this kind of speculation is not enough to defuse the worry. The point is that the consequentialist would be logically committed to chopping up Chuck *if* that were the way to promote the overall good. That in itself seems to be enough to show that there's something serious amiss with consequentialism.

The ethics of rights has a long and complex history, but in that history the writings of the German enlightenment thinker Immanuel Kant (1724–1804) loom large. Kant conceived of ethics primarily in terms of the twin notions of duties and rights. He believed that moral duties and the rights that correspond to them ultimately derive from a fundamental, or governing, duty to act in accordance with, and out of respect for, what he called the *categorical imperative*. If asked why we should respect this imperative, the answer, according to Kant, is that it would be irrational not to do so. The requirements of morality are, fundamentally, requirements of rationality. In its most trenchant version the categorical imperative runs:

> *Act in such a way that you treat humanity, whether in your own person or in the person of any other, always at the same time as an end and never merely as a means to an end.* (Kant 1993, p. 30)

Let us try to unpack what it is Kant is saying here. In conversational English he is saying: "In your conduct always treat yourself and others as ends, not merely as means to an end." What does it mean to treat another person as an end, or as a means to an end? Treating someone as a means implies either that you act selfishly, or that you *use* that person as a vehicle to reach some other goal which is not shared by him or her. Roughly speaking, it means *ignoring* the fact that others have their own goals, dignity, integrity, will and freedom. We can simplify matters somewhat, and combine these features, and say that you treat another as a means when you do not take his or her *interests* as a rational and moral being (sufficiently) into account.

Conversely, treating a person as an end involves taking him or her seriously as an equal human being with interests that ought not to be ignored just to further some other end. Note, by the way, that Kant did not claim that you should treat persons *solely* as ends in themselves. That demand would make it impossible for you to so much as buy a newspaper, because in doing so you would in one way be treating the newsagent a means of satisfying your desires. Kant's position is that you

109

should *also* treat the seller as an end – for instance, by paying the full amount for the paper.

This connects the ethics of rights tradition with an ideal of *moral equality*. Consequentialism is, or can be, one way of trying to respect moral equality. In it, each person's welfare counts for as much as that of any other individual. However, because the focus is on maximizing totals, this is compatible with sacrificing one or some for the greater good. The American philosopher John Rawls (1921–2002), objected to utilitarianism on the grounds that it fails to give equal protection to all: only the abstract "good" counts and we are, in a certain sense, all "means" – or, more vividly, tools – to the end of promoting the good. This is the only sense in which we are "equals" in utilitarianism (Rawls 1971).

The ideal of moral equality expressed or encompassed by Kant's categorical imperative is very different: as rational beings, capable of deliberation and of acting accordingly, we are all equals. The same categorical imperative applies to all, because the laws of rational thought are the same for all rational beings. We therefore owe exactly the same kind of respect to all rational beings. The ethics of rights tradition enshrines this ideal of equality by ascribing certain (equal) rights to each and every one of us.

In ethics courses today Kant is typically set against Mill. Mill represents consequentialism. Kant is by contrast the sternest *deontologist* (from the Greek *dei* = it is right). In his writings Kant tends to shine the spotlight on duties more than rights. However, very little hangs on this. If I have a duty to tell the truth, you have a right to be told the truth. If I have a right not to be attacked, you have a duty to refrain from attacking me, and so on. Barring some fringe cases, we can say that duties and rights are two sides of the same ethical coin.

According to Kant only persons have rights, and in practice that means that only humans have rights. However, some have argued that even non-human animals can be bearers of rights. Thus the American philosopher Tom Regan claims that animals have rights, and should never be treated merely as a means to others' ends.

Rights, according to Regan, belong to beings that can accurately be described as "subjects-of-a-life". Subjects of this kind are psychologically sophisticated: they have desires, beliefs, some form of memory, and the ability, however limited, to anticipate the future. These mental capacities are important because creatures that have them lead *lives that matter to them*. Thus a pet dog that waits for its owner's return from work and prefers one brand of tinned food to another is leading a life that matters to it. In Regan's view, any creature leading a life that matters to it has the right to be treated as an end in itself. We have this right, but so do quite a number of animal species (Regan 1983).

From the basic right to be treated as an end various other rights flow: for example, Regan takes a categorically abolitionist view of animal experimentation and livestock farming. It is wrong to take the life of a healthy animal that does not pose a threat or otherwise harm it no matter what the beneficial consequences may be for others. But the details of Regan's position need not detain us here. The main point to grasp is that he draws the rights boundary with a concept – the "subject-of-a-life" concept – that brings some animals into the group of rights bearers.

For the rest of this chapter we will focus on humans as bearers of rights. However, most of what is said would in principle be applicable to animals, assuming that the animals are included among those beings that are bearers of rights.

From equal moral standing to rights

The ethics of rights tradition, then, can be seen as just one way of fleshing out the ideal of moral equality. Everyone should be treated with equal respect, always. However, this certainly does not mean that we should all have the same level of income, or comparable possessions. It means that we possess identical dignity, value, or worth, and that every one of us has the *right* to be treated as such.

Within the ethics of rights tradition there are other ways of conceptualizing our equal moral worth. The most prominent is the idea of *natural rights*. The word "natural" should not be misunderstood. Its association with biological nature, and again, with that which is self-evident, can easily mislead. What is meant by natural rights is simply *fundamental* rights that need (and in some versions of the idea can have) no further grounding. These fundamental rights are something we all have, simply in virtue of our status as human beings, and not in virtue of our nationality, our efforts, race, sex, religion or any other feature. This is why there is a close affinity between the concept of natural rights and the concept of *human* rights (as the latter are set out, for example, in the UN declaration of human rights.)

Now, an important point: it is one thing to say that we are on the same moral footing, or that we all possess the same moral worth. But it is quite another to say that we all have the same *rights*. Nevertheless, rights seem to be a straightforward expression of our equal worth. By giving – or acknowledging – a fundamental right, say, to your life and possessions, I affirm that your life cannot be sacrificed for the sake of others: you are worth as much as they are, and vice versa. And this returns us to the crucial point of difference between the ethics of rights tradition and consequentialism: the former disputes the latter's idea that morality consists of maximizing welfare come what may. The rights of individuals must be respected, and these rights sometimes block any move toward maximizing welfare.

What is a right?

A good way of conceptualizing rights is to conceive them as follows:

> If a person *P* has a right, R, then:
> (1) *P* is permitted to do R, and
> (2) no one is allowed to interfere with *P* doing R.
> And all this under the condition that
> (3) by doing R, *P* does not violate the rights of other people.

Suppose Angus has the right to healthcare. By (1) He is permitted access to healthcare. By (2) no one is allowed to interfere, for example, with his going to hospital. Now for a crucial distinction: is the right in question *negative* or *positive*? A negative right involves that no one is allowed to obstruct Angus from going to hospital and seeking a doctor. However, no one is morally obliged to support Angus. His possession of this negative right does not entail that others are obliged to build a hospital, serve as doctors, give him medicine, and so on. It merely entails that others must refrain from doing something, namely obstruct Angus' pursuit of healthcare.

A *positive* right is, very often, much stronger. It entails that others are obliged to help Angus. So we need to add a fourth item to the list when we are talking about positive rights. Where positive rights are at issue:

> (4) others have a duty to assist *P* in doing/achieving R.

This simple, yet highly significant distinction is all too often overlooked. Furthermore, we need to pay close attention to (3). Suppose Angus does have a right to healthcare. This does not entail that Angus has the right to run over Bonnie on his way to hospital, because Bonnie also has a right to her life and limbs.

In theory, many things can be claimed as rights: life, liberty, food and shelter, the opportunity to take a holiday ... the list is pretty open-ended. Historically, the ethics of rights tradition has been quite moderate in its claims and concentrated on basic necessities: life, liberty and the pursuit of happiness, understood in falling degrees from the negative to the positive – e.g. you might have some (modest) claims against others to ensure your survival. Nevertheless, your life and liberty is mainly negatively protected. On the other hand, in recent years, especially in the human rights field, there has been much more emphasis on positive rights.

How do rights do their job?

The American jurisprudent Ronald Dworkin (1931–2013) introduced a powerful metaphor to explain how rights work which we will expand on here. Imagine that all of our various claims on others ("Do that for me", "Don't interfere with me doing this", "Assist me with the other") form a deck of cards (Dworkin 1984). Some cards have more moral value than others. If one of your friends asks you to help her out for a few hours because her baby is sick and she cannot afford a babysitter and another asks you to come over to chat, then, very probably, the first friend's "card" will have higher value. Rights function as *trumps* in this card game: they override all other claims. If you have a positive right to medical assistance in a certain situation, that right trumps other claims, including the claim that your local municipality could save a lot of money by not treating patients who will not or cannot pay for themselves.

Trumps, then, express the basic idea in the ethics of rights tradition that individuals have some very strong claims against others, and crucially a moral claim not to be sacrificed for the greater good. If the surgeon asks Chuck to give up his organs to save the lives of five people, Chuck is entitled to refuse. It would be very nice, in fact heroic, of him to make this sacrifice. It may also be true that total human well-being would be hugely increased by the organ harvest. But he has a right *not* to do so. His right to life functions as a trump against the claims of the ailing five.

Naturally, the deck cannot be a collection *only* of trumps. That would result in social deadlock. On the other hand, we would probably wish to claim more than just one trump – more, say, than the negative right to life. The card game metaphor with an emphasis on trumps nicely illustrates the logic of a rights discourse. It also illustrates a fundamental problem: what are we to do when two trumps are played? We will return to this below.

Since not every card in the deck is a trump, there will be some situations where trumps do not come into play. Does this mean that *morality* does not come into play? After all, if our basic moral standing is expressed in rights, and rights function as trumps, it looks as though any situation that does not involve trumps does not involve morality. Those in the ethics of rights tradition disagree on this matter. Some would indeed be prepared to say that insofar as no rights are involved in a situation, there is no "moral truth" to be found. Morality takes a holiday.

This view does at least have the merit of capturing many people's (incidentally, strongly anti-consequentialist) intuition that some areas of our lives have to be free of moral directives. But others would say that, once trumps are out of play other, admittedly less authoritative, moral reasoning takes over, including quite possibly consequentialist reasoning. Thus your feeling (if you have it) that it would be wrong to pursue your social life rather than assisting a friend without the money for a babysitter need not be based on deontological respect for rights. For all that has been said, it could be grounded in a consequentialist belief that it would be unethical, in the situation at hand, not to do the thing that contributes most to net welfare.

It remains the case, however, that the thrust of the ethics of rights is toward the view that, once rights are out of the picture, "true" or "mandatory" morality is at rest. This is definitely not to deny that unselfish contributions to the welfare of others are commendable or praiseworthy. The point is merely that it is not *morally obligatory* to make such contributions.

Some problems with rights

Rights do not always conform as neatly with common-sense moral beliefs as they do in the case of Chuck. In this last section, we will discuss two kinds of case where there is divergence.

The morality of killing: Some believe that in extreme situations, such as war, ordinary morality is suspended. Probably this is at least psychologically true. However, it is controversial to say that the demands of morality are shelved just because the circumstances are adversarial. Indeed this seems to undermine the very point of rights and morally guided action.

In war we often encounter the problem of *collateral damage* – in plain words, the killing of innocent civilians. Warfare almost inevitably means that we kill or maim innocent people. How can this be reconciled with the fact that these innocents have an absolute right to life?

The radical answer is to maintain that the killing of innocents violates people's basic rights, so there is no justification for collateral damage, and hence for any warfare that involves it. But such *pacifism* appeals to very few since most people find it intuitively right to defend yourself against an aggressor, e.g. if your country is attacked. The human capacity to inflict grievous harm is truly frightening and in the light of that most find it ethically justified to defend yourself or those that are innocent.

Very few advocates of the ethics of rights have been pacifists, and a variety of attempts to solve the rights-in-war conundrum have been made. The most important is the *doctrine of double effect*. This is the doctrine that it is sometimes morally permissible to harm, or even kill, people, if the harm or death is "foreseen" but "not intended" by the agent. Of course, this doctrine doesn't licence foreseen harm come what may. The agent's intention must be to do something that is in some sense out-weighs the regrettable, foreseen harm.

A couple of examples will help. Doctors sometimes give terminally ill patients pain killers such as morphine which are known to hasten the patient's death. If the intent, however, is to relieve pain, double effect can be invoked to explain why this is an acceptable practice. Occasionally, pregnant women develop uterine cancer. When they do, the normal clinical response is to surgically remove the womb, and unless it is at an advanced stage of development the foetus will die. The Catholic Church regards this as an exception to its prohibition on abortion on the grounds that it is not an intentional killing of the foetus. The death of the foetus is a foreseen outcome of the procedure, but the surgeon's intention is to save the woman.

Returning to the subject of war, collateral damage can be looked at through the prism of double effect. Thus, it might be suggested that the intention of the 2003 "shock and awe" bombings of Baghdad was to hit military targets, although it was anticipated that civilian deaths – men, women and children – would follow. This rendered the attacks acceptable.

Critics maintain that this way of conceptualizing moral issues is incompatible with the ethics of rights. It simply seems too convenient that people's rights suddenly present no obstacle when the harm being done to them is merely foreseen, but not intended. Suppose we dump dangerous nuclear waste in the sea, and people protest, saying it will harm people in the future. It is hardly an excuse to say that we "only foresee" and "do not intend" harm. Here, defenders of the doctrine of double effect will say: "Ah! But dumping nuclear waste in this example is illegitimate because the dumping does not have a sufficiently productive, intended outcome. The goal must outweigh the harm done." But it is arguable that this only serves to deepen the difficulty. The response seems to be saying that a person's rights can be put to one side only when action infringing them leads to a better outcome. This appears to be a straightforward example of consequentialist thought. At this point the whole rights-edifice then seems to be redundant, if not downright self-defeating.

Conflicts of rights: Another problem for the ethics of rights-tradition arises when rights conflict with one another. So far we have concentrated on the basic right to life, but of course other rights are usually added to this. One familiar right in the ethics of rights tradition is the right to *bodily integrity*. This is related to, but differs from, the right to life. It protects you from wanton injury and maiming by others of the sort that does not kill you. Let us assume that people have this right to bodily integrity. Adapting a famous example of Thomas Nagel's (1986), imagine that you and your friend survive a car crash. However, your friend is in dire need of medical treatment. In fact, he will die very soon if he does not get to a hospital, and of course the car you were driving in is in pieces. You enter a house, asking for help, but frighten the elderly woman who lives there and she runs into the bathroom to hide, locking the door behind her. The old lady is also the owner of a mint condition Ferrari Testarossa which will surely get your friend to hospital in good time. You decide to grab the lady's grandchild and twist the child's arm, forcing the woman to hand over the key to the car.

The problem is, of course, that you are violating at least one right (the innocent child's right to bodily integrity) to safeguard another man's right (your friend's right to life.) Intuitively, the way to resolve this conflict is to compare the gravity of each violation. However, this is not a satisfactory course. First, it implies that we *can* sacrifice one person's interests in order to promote another's. This is exactly the kind of move that the ethics of rights was devised prevent. Second, if we are to compare violations, we need a measure of gravity. But that leads us on to a slippery slope which leads back to the measurement of *welfare*. After all, what other plausible criterion could you use to measure the gravity of a rights violation? But this reiterates the problem we encountered when we discussed the doctrine of double effect: that under the fine veneer of rights lurks the quicksand of consequentialism.

Some proponents of the ethics of rights opt for a radical solution: they insist that we should not allow comparisons of welfare to enter our deliberations. This position is often accompanied by the claim that what matters is not what happens as seen from a point of view "outside" the concrete moral situation, where we can make judgments such as "a minor or major infringement of rights", or "the total sum of rights violations", and then opt for the lesser of two or more evils. Rather, what is morally relevant is only how *you* behave, *not* what happens in the big picture. It is *your* duty to make sure that you do not infringe anyone's rights, but it is not your duty to act so as to minimize the number of violations, or maximize the number of rights-respecting acts. As the American libertarian philosopher Robert Nozick (1938–2002), a leading modern proponent of the ethics of rights, once put it, there is no place for a "utilitarianism of rights".

This might solve the immediate theoretical problem. But it comes at a high price. For common sense surely dictates that it is often *morally* better to violate a "small" right in order to prevent the violation of a "bigger" right by another person. It would surely be morally acceptable to borrow a rowing boat without permission when by doing so one can prevent the drowning of three children. Perhaps common sense is wrong here. However, the notion that in borrowing a rowing boat without permission you commit a greater moral wrong than you would in allowing three children to die, seems to fetishize rights at the expense of human decency. Moreover, if one of the points of the ethics of rights tradition is to express a robust kind of *respect* for people, it seems odd to ignore the plight of people in serious jeopardy in the name of an abstract moral concept like the concept of rights.

We have drawn a picture of the ethics of rights where there is no possible compromise or overlap between that theory and consequentialism. However, maybe future philosophical studies will show that the border line between these theories is rather porous. The British philosopher Derek Parfit (2011) has recently developed some ingenious arguments to that effect. For instance, insofar, or because, an agent is not irrational by giving up a "lesser" right (e.g. his ownership or property rights to a rowboat) in order for a "higher" right to be fulfilled (e.g. saving the lives of the drowning children), one is not using that agent merely as a means when one takes his boat without his permission. Maybe some of the major ethical theories are indeed "climbing the same mountain from different slopes", to use Parfit's phrase. However, Parfit's arguments are highly controversial and there is no consensus in the philosophical community that he is right.

Key points

- The ethics of rights, just like consequentialism, has strengths and weaknesses. On the upside, it is an intuitively much more palatable way of fleshing out the ideal of moral equality and respect – or equal human worth – than the equivalent idea in consequentialism that "everybody's interests are to be taken into account, but this might mean sacrificing *your* interests". Moreover, it creates a kind of haven where the demands of morality do not intrude – or at least not with full force – and this is in accordance with many people's experience of moral life. Finally, it captures our firm intuitions in cases such as the one of Chuck.

- On the downside, the ethics of rights tradition faces a dilemma. It could allow for comparisons when rights-claims collide, but this threatens to undermine the distinctiveness of rights theory and turn the ethics of rights into a circular form of consequentialism. Alternatively, the ethics of rights could uphold a strict rights-and-duties scheme offering no place for comparisons, but this would

117

threaten to distance it from common sense. Arguably, it would also involve fetishizing the concept of rights instead of caring about and, in that rather different sense, respecting people.

- A third alternative would be insist that rights and duties guide human conduct up to a point, but allow that when rights are in conflict comparisons are appropriate and perfectly proper. It could also be agreed that when we are in reasonable doubt (or when there are no rights at issue) we should be guided by some sort of consequentialism. Such a pluralistic theory will not appeal to purist advocates of the ethics of rights. However, it seems to overcome many of the difficulties philosophers have identified in the discussion of the ethics of rights tradition.

- Rights theorists might retort that morality is not neat and clear-cut. Sometimes we face hard choices. Ethics – not as a result of our incompetency or lack of a precise moral theory – is sometimes unavoidably tragic. It does rather seem, however, that the ethics of rights-tradition conjures moral tragedies where none exist. By insisting on the sanctity of minor rights, protecting relatively marginal interests, it allows *much* worse tragedies to happen. This flies in the face of common sense.

References

Dworkin, Ronald (1984): Rights as Trumps. In: Jeremy Waldron (ed.) *Theories of Rights*, pp. 153-67. Oxford: Oxford University Press.

Foot, Philippa (1967): The Problem of Abortion and the Doctrine of Double Effect. *Oxford Review* 5: 5-15.

Kagan, Shelly (1998): *Normative Ethics*. Boulder CO: Westview Press.

Kant, Immanuel (1993): *Grounding for the Metaphysics of Morals* (translated by James W. Ellington). Indianapolis IN: Hackett Publishing Company. [First issued 1785]

Nagel, Thomas (1986): *The View from Nowhere*. Oxford: Oxford University Press.

Parfit, Derek (2011): *On what Matters*. Oxford: Oxford University Press.

Rawls, John (1971): *A Theory of Justice*. London: Oxford University Press.

Regan Tom (1983): *The case for animal rights*. Berkeley & Los Angeles CA: University of California Press.

Further reading

Harman, Gilbert (1977): *The Nature of Morality: An Introduction to Ethics*. Oxford: Oxford University Press.

Kagan, Shelly (1989): *The Limits of Morality*. Oxford: Oxford University Press.

Kagan, Shelly (1998): *Normative Ethics*. Boulder CO: Westview Press.

Smart, J.J.C. & Williams, Bernard (1973): *Utilitarianism: For and against*. Cambridge UK: Cambridge University Press.

Tännsjö, Torbjörn (2002): *Understanding ethics: An Introduction to Moral Theory*. Edinburgh: Edinburgh University Press.

Thompson, J.J. (1991): Self-Defense. *Philosophy and Public Affairs* 20 (4): 283-310.

8
Virtue Ethics

In this chapter we examine virtue ethics and situational ethics. In important respects these two approaches to ethical theory are very different from the positions we have looked at elsewhere in the book. The consequentialist, contractarian and rights-based theorists share many assumptions about the purpose and potential of ethical theory which are revised, or rejected outright, by the virtue ethicist and the situational ethicist. These assumptions can be hard to pin down, but they basically revolve around the idea that morality can be captured in a set of principles, or rules of conduct. By contrast, virtue ethics, and perhaps especially situational ethics, proposes that we should not be focusing exclusively on right action. We must also remember that ethics should give us an answer to the question: what sort of person should I be? Situational ethicists, equally unimpressed by the principalist programme, suggest that intersubjective relations between persons provide the fundamental key to morality.

Imagine you have a serious disease requiring highly sophisticated surgery. The chances are 50:50 that you will survive the procedure. You are obviously rather worried and in need both of reassurance, hope and the feeling that others are concerned about you and will do whatever they can to help you. One of the people best placed to do this is the family doctor who diagnosed the disease. She has known you since you were a child and you trust her. As far as you know she is currently taking care of her patients at the clinic back home while you lie in bed at the hospital ward on the other side of town. Suddenly there is a knock on the door and she steps in. She has brought you a soy latte, your favourite drink, and some magazines. She sits down and begins talking. After an hour or so you feel much better. She has explained the procedures to you and, without neglecting the risks, given you hope that everything will turn out to the best. But first and foremost she has given you a feeling of well-being and gratitude to her for taking the time to come and see you. You feel less alone in facing the unknown future. As she gets ready to leave you thank her for coming and tell her how much her visit has meant to you.

Probably, most people will think the doctor does the right thing here. However, different moral theories or perspectives will give rather different account of *why* the doctor's choices and actions are right in a case like this. So, let us see how the doctor would explain and justify her actions focusing on *consequences* (i.e. as a consequentialist); on *rights* (i.e. as a proponent of the ethics of rights); and then on *virtues* (i.e. as a virtue ethicist).

Consequences: "I had to come. Having evaluated all relevant scenarios, I discovered that this was the way I could contribute the most to total happiness in the world. But it was a close call between you and a homeless guy, who needed attention as well. What turned things to your advantage was the effect that my visit will have, indirectly, on your family when they come to see you and find that you are in a better mood."

Rights: "I had to come. It was my duty. Actually I would much rather have spent these hours on the beach, but that would have been wrong: it would have been following my inclinations, whereas taking the utmost care of my patients is my duty as a doctor. In actual fact, things became clearer to me when I realized that I actually do not like you very much. The fact that I really did not want to come only served to make it more apparent that I had an obligation to do so, thus fulfilling my duties towards humanity in general."

Virtues: "I had to come. I believe a good human seeks to take care of that part of the other person's life that they have influence on. As your doctor I know your situation better than most, so who better than me to come and seek to comfort you? I sincerely try to be a decent human being, and visiting you seemed the decent thing to do. Being the person I am – and that I want to be – not to mention my function as your family doctor, I couldn't do otherwise."

Virtue ethicists believe their theory captures some essential features of morality which neither consequentialism nor the ethics of rights can accommodate. First and foremost, they believe we need to focus on the *good person*. We should not always ask: what ought I to do? Rather, we should seek to answer that question indirectly by answering another one, namely: what *sort of person* should I be? Furthermore, an adequate conception of such a person will stress *virtues* (understood as personal qualities).

Such virtues can be conceptualized in two ways, both of which are in play in the case. When the doctor says that she could not do otherwise, given the person she is and wants to be, we can think of virtues as something had by all decent or virtuous people. But the doctor also says that her *function*, or role, as a medical practitioner makes some virtues, or personal qualities, especially important for her. Obviously, we are not all doctors. We work in various fields, in different jobs. In view of this, virtue ethics acknowledges that there are some *function-specific* virtues – e.g. the virtues of a good doctor, nurse, or craftsman. Let us try to unpack the theoretical rationale behind this line of reasoning.

Although it was in academic circles relatively dormant through much of the twentieth century, virtue ethics is one of the great traditions in normative ethics. Indeed many theorists take the three great schools of normative ethics to be deontology (what we have called the rights tradition), consequentialism, and virtue ethics. Unsurprisingly, then, virtue ethics has a long history. It can be found in the writings of prominent ancient Greek philosophers, and especially in the treatises of Aristotle (385–322 BC) who is a key historical figure in ethics. Through the work of Aristotle, and its development by theologians like Thomas Aquinas, the tradition of virtue ethics remained alive and robust until at least the late medieval period.

Three notions used in virtue ethics

According to one of its contemporary proponents, Rosalind Hursthouse, one needs to understand three concepts to get to grips with virtue ethics (Hursthouse 2012). These are the concepts of virtue (in ancient Greek *arête)*, happiness (*eudaimonia*), and practical wisdom (*phronesis*). Let us take these in turn.

Virtues
Virtues are character traits which consistently guide a person's actions, thoughts, feelings, desires, and so on, whenever the virtue is relevant. They form part of a *mind-set*. Hence, virtues are more deep-seated and multifaceted than a disposition to act in a certain way for some mainly external reason, such as avoiding cheating other people out of fear of retribution. Genuine possession of the virtue of honesty, for example, will bring with it repercussions across a range of situations, directions of thought, and decisions, for the honest person:

> *An honest person's reasons and choices with respect to honest and dishonest actions reflect her views about honesty and truth – but of course such views manifest themselves with respect to other actions, and to emotional reactions as well. Valuing honesty as she does, she chooses, where possible to work with honest people, to have honest friends, to bring up her children to be honest. She disapproves of, dislikes, deplores dishonesty, is not amused by certain tales of*

123

chicanery, despises or pities those who succeed by dishonest means rather than thinking they have been clever, is unsurprised, or pleased (as appropriate) when honesty triumphs, is shocked or distressed when those near and dear to her do what is dishonest and so on. (Hursthouse 2012, section 2)

Hence, a virtue is not just some isolated, somewhat random, tendency to give a couple of dollars to a charity every now and then. A truly generous, or compassionate, person is a person who lives and thinks always, or very nearly so, as a generous or compassionate person. Now, different virtue ethicists offer different catalogues of the virtues. There is no agreement on the list. Typical candidates, however, include things as honesty, courage, justice, temperance, and compassion. Many virtue ethicists take their cue from Aristotle and define virtues in terms of what he called a "golden mean", or middle way, between two best-avoided extremes. For example, courage is the middle course between timidity, or cowardice, and rash impulsiveness.

For Aristotle himself the most important virtues are justice, fortitude, courage, liberality, magnificence, magnanimity, and temperance. This list demonstrates a notable feature of virtues: their historical and cultural specificity. Virtues arise and make sense in particular social settings and at particular times. The relative importance attached by people to one virtue, as against another, may well change over time, or from place to place.

One question this raises in virtue ethics is whether the observed variation is *ineradicable*. Universalist virtue ethicists argue that it is. The list of "real" virtues, according to them, is at least relatively stable and uniform across time and cultures. The communitarian, on the other hand, argues that the virtues are stubbornly relative to specific communities at specific times. (This last incarnation of virtue ethics is connected with the political theory also known as communitarianism, touched upon in chapter 10 of this book.)

Quite how we (or others) are to arrive at a list of virtues will be discussed later. Suffice it to say, for now, that most of the items on most lists generally strike most people as *admirable*: they are traits or dispositions that most of us admire when we see them in other people, and we might also feel proud when we exhibit them ourselves.

For the proponent of virtue ethics, moral challenges typically involve clashes between competing virtues – but not conflicting rights, or incompatible recommendations as to the best way to maximize the good. In the case described in the beginning of this chapter the doctor has clearly weighed up loyalty and her personal relationship when she decided to attend to your needs rather than a stranger's (which could be a question of justice or mercy). She has also decided to give more weight to loyalty and your shared relationship than other virtues, such as conscientious care of her own private practice. However, it is not necessarily easy to make such moral decisions, based on the virtues. What, for instance, if compassion is incompatible with justice, or honesty (telling your aunt that her cookies are in fact awful) over compassion (sparing your aunt)? It looks as though the virtues can be in competition, and given this it is insufficient simply to have virtues: one must also be able to prioritize them properly in your conduct: in other words, one needs practical wisdom.

Practical wisdom

Practical wisdom is part and parcel of the make-up of the truly virtuous person. It is an essential manager of the virtues. We can imagine someone with the virtue of generosity who, lacking practical wisdom, gives money away in such an undisciplined manner that he or she is unable to exercise other virtues such as justice. It may be that the person in question cannot repay a debt as a result of previous generosity.

Of course, one could insist that *genuine* generosity is a mean, and that undisciplined benefactors are therefore not generous, but extravagant. However, finding the mean of single virtues and balancing them against other virtues are acts of practical wisdom, just like the act of balancing between the twin extremes representing deformations of single virtues. This makes it meaningful to distinguish between the virtues *per se* and wisdom. Now, wisdom is indeed *learned*, not something people are born with. You might be born extremely intelligent, but without practice and experience you cannot be wise. Moral wisdom requires, or consists of, what is sometimes called "situational appreciation", i.e. the ability to identify what is morally relevant, and what is irrelevant, in a given situation. This ability is not something that can be learned "from the armchair", and it cannot be reduced to a simple principle or set of rules that can be learned in the abstract. It is hard not to underestimate the role wisdom plays in virtue ethics. Indeed, the label "wisdom ethics" is apt, given that wisdom plays such a crucial role in the decisions of the virtuous agent.

The Greek philosopher Hierocles had his fictional character Scholasticus say that it is better to learn how to swim *before* one ventures into the water for the first time (Hegel 1991, p. 34). Virtue ethicists would appreciate the ironic wisdom encapsulated in this thought: displaying the virtues and living morally is something which needs to be learned and practiced, and for this we need good role models, moral education. We need to become both virtuous and wise.

Happiness
Happiness is what one attains through proper exercise of the virtues. It is necessary to think of this happiness in a slightly technical way. The original Greek word of which it is a translation, "eudaimonia", is more accurately translated *flourishing*. Things flourish when they perform their function well and thus fulfil their potential. Different kinds of thing have different potentials. Under good care, a house plant can flourish. Leopards can also flourish, but in a different way, obviously. Human beings flourish, or achieve happiness in the ancient Greek sense, by fulfilling potentials lacked by other animals. Aristotle thought that our distinctive potential, or function, is to reason. For him, we flourish when we reason well – when we live in accordance with reason.

It is worth comparing the virtue ethicist's conception of happiness with the theories of the good encountered in chapter 3. Plainly, eudaimonic happiness is not a Benthamite experience of pleasure and the absence of pain. Nor is it preference-satisfaction. It might be suggested that there is an overlap inasmuch as eudaimonia involves the satisfaction of preferences to be virtuous and do virtuous things. However, it is the exercise of these preferences, not their satisfaction, which matters in virtue ethics. Nor is happiness, as conceived by the virtue ethicist, the same as the possession of objective goods of the kind that appear in the perfectionist's list. Rather, on most understandings of virtue ethics, happiness is a thoroughly *moralized* conception of the instrumentally good. What is truly good for you simply *is* the morally good. Despite appearances, there is no happiness to be had in being evil, bad or unjust. Thus the gap between the purely self-interested good and the morally good is therefore straddled by the eudaimonic conception of happiness. Virtue is the only way to flourish, and the happy life just *is* a moral life. A person lacking virtue may *feel* happy, but that feeling is always an illusion. He or she is not truly happy, in the sense of flourishing, according to virtue ethics.

For some this is a very attractive conception of the good, precisely because it collapses the distinction between self-interest and morality: prudential and moral reasons cease to diverge. Your motivation to be moral is that, this way, you will flourish. The big questions here centre on the happiness being promised. This needs to be sufficiently like the happiness we ordinarily seek and enjoy to be indisputably desirable, yet sufficiently unlike it to make room for the possibility that you cannot be happy, in the requisite sense, unless you are virtuous.

A final question is whether the virtues *guarantee* happiness. In some versions of virtue ethics they do – virtue is a sufficient condition for happiness. Other versions, virtue is a necessary, but not sufficient condition of happiness – external factors, such as resources, are also needed.

Virtue ethics and the question of right action

As we mentioned at the start of the chapter, principalist moral theories focus on the first-person ethical question: what ought I to *do*? They are designed to provide *criteria* of rightness: rules specifying exactly what an agent ought to do in particular circumstances. On this approach the ideal moral theory will be like an instruction manual or handbook. Virtue ethics is preoccupied with a significantly different question, namely: who ought I to be? And the answer, naturally, is that one should be a *virtuous* person. The virtuous person is variously described as a "person of character", or integrity, or simply as a good person. Let us look briefly at some of the reasons why virtue ethicists want us to focus on the virtuous person rather than criteria of rightness.

One reason contemporary proponents of virtue ethics want us to concentrate on the virtuous person is dissatisfaction with the sometimes very formal, "faceless" and abstract nature of approaches such as consequentialism and the ethics of rights. Take the ethics of rights. Faced with an ethically challenging situation, the rights theorist will usually need to put to one side *any* particular trait, preference, inclination, or sympathy in order to reach a "truly universal" point of view from which a moral judgment can be made. Similarly, the utilitarian has a restless concern with the greatest good for all which tends to obliterate all personal concerns (unless of course those concerns happen to foster the greatest good for all). It is small wonder that some feel alienated by these mind-sets. It is easy to develop doubts: they say this is *moral*, but is it *good*? Is this really the *kind of person* I would want to be? Would I, indeed, want *other* people to look at the world that way?

A more radical complaint is that abstract, principled theories are, at the end of the day, morally *bad*, not only for person trying to live out their values, but all things considered. Thus some virtue ethicists have stressed that trying to subsume all *concrete* ethical situations under a general rule or principle is likely to distort our perception of what is really going on. We lose something valuable when we try to abstract from the actual and concrete circumstances of an ethically challenging situation, it is said. Other virtue theorists have made a more historical point. They have argued that without an understanding of the virtues – an understanding we have lost, partly because we have been preoccupied with questions of rightness rather than virtue – the application of the abstract moral principles is bound to be blind and counterproductive vis-à-vis the goal of doing what is ethically best in the situation.

Another complaint commonly voiced by virtue ethicists is that modern ethics has lost any connection with the *good life*. This, of course, is related to the first argument. Think again of the ideal Kantian or utilitarian agent. It seems that their lives could be very drab, or even quite unpleasant, without being any the less moral for all that. In these theories *moral* life seems therefore to be utterly divorced from the *good life*. The ancient Greeks would have had trouble understanding this. They generally thought of virtuous living as a good life. They would have been puzzled – perhaps even dismayed – by the idea that, in an important sense, morality is a form of self-denial, or at any rate self-sacrifice.

Sympathy with the virtue ethicists understanding of the close connection between the right and the good need not catapult us into ethical egoism and the contractarian conception of the ethical examined in chapter 6. Here we can only touch on why, but basically the difference between the two approaches is as follows. The contractarian builds morality on a foundation of non-moral materials. The key idea is that the device of a contract can be used to show how morality emerges from, and is justified by, the fact of self-interest. By contrast, in virtue ethics the notion of a non-moral foundation plays no role. Nor is a contract invoked. The idea is not that calculated self-interest generates morality by agreement – or, more accurately, by a deal you will be held to. Rather it is that our self-interest is infused, from the very beginning, with ethical character. No contract is needed to get morality out of human nature, because that nature is ethical all the way down.

Virtue ethics can, then, be regarded as a theory which strikes a balance between, on the one hand, selfless positions such as consequentialism and rights theory and, on the other hand, the egoism of contractarianism. For many proponents of virtue ethics, their theory is just this. It shows the connection between morality and the good life without wholly collapsing into egoism. It also explains why we should be moral without demanding that we become "slaves of morality".

It is hard to overemphasize the importance of this last point. According to the virtue ethicist, neither consequentialism nor rights theory can provide a persuasive answer to the thorny old question: why should I be moral? Virtue ethics has a ready answer: the *moral* life is a good life – a life in which the agent is happy and flourishes. In the fully virtuous person there is no clash of inclination and moral decency. You should be moral, not because universal reason, rights, or utility dictates so, but because only in that way will you enjoy the good life. Advocates of virtue ethics claim that this is an important advantage over consequentialism and rights theory.

Criticisms of virtue ethics

Having thus described some of the central claims of virtue ethics, it is time to look at some of the alleged weaknesses of virtue ethics. Let us begin by looking briefly at what has become known as the "circularity problem". A number of critics have claimed that virtue ethics lacks a criterion of rightness. This is a complicated issue, but the gist of the problem is that the argument seems to be constructed like this: Follow the virtues because they are morally good. Why are the virtues morally good: Because they lead to a flourishing life. Why do they lead to a flourishing life: Because they are morally good.

This is from an explanatory point of view obviously not a satisfactory answer. It seems that we are stuck in a circle: the virtues are good because they are virtues. Various ways out of this circle have been proposed, and it is a topic of continuing interest in contemporary debate over virtue ethics.

Scholars working in other traditions are unlikely to be persuaded that virtue ethics can provide a fully satisfying response here. What they want is for virtue ethics to provide a non-circular, independent and convincing criterion of rightness – or, as it might be said, they want to be shown a feature of moral situations which can serve as a foundation for moral assessment. For utilitarians this feature is simply the propensity of the various acts available in the situation to produce good and/or minimize bad.

For proponents of the ethics of rights it could be the person's obeying the categorical imperative, or acting out of duty. What is it for the virtue ethicist – the existence in the situation of elements that allow us to display the virtues? That would mean that bad situations are in one sense good, because they allow us to display virtue. Most of us would be somewhat wary of such a view, surely. Moreover, it would point to some feature *outside* the agent (and hence, something *apart* from the virtues) that made situations "good-apt". However, in the end this would mean that the virtues are not basic. Some readers will no doubt wish to object that this is a general problem for all moral theories. After all, one might ask the utilitarian: what is so good about the good that we *need* to promote it? And it would appear that similar questions can be used to embarrass all moral theories. But this is to miss the point of the critique of virtue ethics.

Few contemporary philosophers believe we can give a satisfying explanation of morality that is free of a starting point one just has to accept – much as one just has to accept certain axioms in order to get mathematics going. The utilitarian can say that the world becomes a better place as it comes to contain more pleasure and less pain. Few would be inclined to say that more pain and less pleasure is *good*, and furthermore, the rightness of actions – whether they promote the good – is defined in terms of something that is independent of goodness itself, namely whether they promote pleasure and minimizes pain. To this the virtue ethicist can point to the flourishing life that following the virtues will lead to, both for others to the extent that they are affected by the actions of the virtue ethicist and for the virtue ethicist herself. None the less many theorists press the criticism of circular reasoning against virtue ethics.

This is connected with another criticism of virtue ethics. Since virtues are at least partially defined in terms of historically contingent circumstances and practices (e.g. the value of physical courage is somewhat less in Athens today than it was in the days of the ancient Greeks) there is a risk that our catalogue of virtues will simply be the mirror of local particularities and prejudices. But morality should be a critic, not a mirror, of the way we conduct ourselves, or so the complaint goes. Some virtue ethicists are content to embrace relativism. Their reaction to this criticism is to deny that moral thinking can be critical in the sense presupposed. They sometimes insist that there is no vantage point, outside of our moral practices, from which we can criticize our morality. A more robust rejoinder involves rejection of the claim that the virtues are necessarily culturally relative. Courage has various *manifestations*, certainly. In a judge working in a corrupt country and in a schoolboy it is expressed quite differently. But this doesn't demonstrate that courage is a collection of culturally determined virtues. In all the cases there is just one virtue in play. It is simply that this single virtue has different implications and reveals itself in variety of ways.

Another well-known problem for virtue ethics revolves around the role of *luck* in the formation of an individual's moral character. The virtuous person displays a developed capacity for moral insight and admirable moral habits. But clearly not everyone has the luck to live in circumstances where such insights and habits can be developed. Should we then condemn such persons for their lack of virtue? Again, if the development of moral character depends in part on luck, should we praise the virtuous? Admittedly, this problem arises for other normative theories. We will also see something very like it being marshalled by Rawls against desert-based theories of distributive justice in chapter 9. But the problem is perhaps particularly troubling for the virtue ethicist, because the virtues are the *basis* of morality. One might be a good utilitarian or contractualist, even though one's "moral character" is rather flawed. But since "character" is so basic for virtue ethics, it can seem that virtue ethics not only condemns certain actions, but also certain *persons*, simply because their "character" is not "virtuous".

In the light of these and similar criticisms, some theorists shy away from the label "virtue ethicist". They accept that virtue *theory* has something important to add to existing normative frameworks, with its focus on the moral individual, on moral character, and on habits, moral education, and so forth. They would be less willing to proclaim that virtue ethics provides a comprehensive account of the ethical. It is hard not to agree that virtue theory has much of value to offer. The actual moral person, with moral sensibilities, imagination, traits, does seem to be overlooked, or given little attention, in principalist ethical theories, and this does seem regrettable. Hence, virtue theory surely has a place in philosophical ethics. Of course some believe that the criticisms of virtue ethics can be dealt with, and that virtue ethics is therefore a full-blown alternative to competing normative theories in its own right. Hopefully, you are now better equipped to make up your own mind on that question.

Situational ethics

We will end by noting a position that shares certain aspects with virtue ethics, but can also be seen as an alternative to virtue ethics. This alternative is known as the ethics of responsibility, or (the name we shall use) *situational ethics*. Situational ethics have certain features in common with virtue ethics. It relies on the idea that we have obligations towards each other (and in some cases to other alleged ethical subjects, e.g. animals or nature) simply because we coexist. The idea is that ethics is, in a sense, founded on the *relation* between human beings, or between human beings and nature. The Danish theologian K. E. Løgstrup (1905–1981) has expressed it thus:

> *The individual is never involved with another human being without having in her hand some of the other person's life ... We are each other's world and destiny ... With our bare attitude towards each other we shape the life-worlds of each other ... This phenomenon is highly disturbing.* (Løgstrup 1991, p. 25 [our translation])

For Løgstrup responsibility immediately reveals itself when we recognize the interdependent nature of human existence. For the French philosopher Immanuel Levinás (1906–1995) the experience of responsibility is closely tied to the experience of the face of the other human being (Levinas 1991), whereas the German philosopher Hans

131

Jonas (1903–1993) maintains that our technological powers give us a distinct sense of responsibility to humans and the rest of nature both now and in the future (Jonas 1984).

Of course, the positions of these three philosophers differ significantly. However, they agree that it is a central task of ethical thinking to point to the unavoidable responsibility we have for other human beings. In their view, as the passage from Løgstrup shows, we are always and already placed in relationships which oblige us to decide whether to use our power over another human being to benefit that being or to benefit ourselves.

The central ethical task thus becomes to realize the responsibility bestowed upon you and figure out how to exercise it properly. This kind of ethical thinking can therefore be understood as a bottom-up approach to ethics. It is the actual meeting with other human beings and the context in which the meeting takes place that confers upon ethical action its legitimacy and, to a certain extent, content. By contrast, utilitarianism and especially deontology can be viewed as top-down approaches in which ethical principles, deducted or rationalized from a theoretical standpoint, infuse the situation we are in with ethical content.

From a Løgstrupian perspective it makes little sense to ask about ethical action outside the concrete situation. Only in an actual situation can "the ethical action" be incarnated as the action which, in that situation, promises to be the best way to respond to the need of the other. The only demand that can be made prior to this is that the ethical action as such should have the other as the centre of the action. One cannot be ethical and, at the same time, wonder: "what's in it for me?" In ethical action there is an unconscious act of self-forgetting that allows the other to take centre-stage.

Philosophers working within this framework of situational ethics thus tend to be rather apprehensive when talk turns to ethical guidelines and advice. They see the ethical nature of human relationships as an integral part of being human – an "existential" part of it, to use a philosophical expression. And because it is part of human nature to be ethical, it is part of human existence to take responsibility for incarnating the ethical action to the best of one's ability in the myriad encounters one has during a lifetime.

The flexibility built into this way of thinking about ethics, as compared, say, with Kant's approach to morality is an obvious advantage. (We are thinking of the problem we saw Kant has with lying in chapter 4). It is the person in front of me and the context that she is in that can help me understand how best to take care of her right here and now. I do not have to check whether the principle underlying my actions can be universalized, or whether my act will increase the total quantity of welfare in the world. I can focus on the human being in front of me and seek to be worthy of the ethical responsibility that comes with human life.

Serious objections have been made to situational ethics. One is that it risks turning ethical actions in to arbitrary interpretations of situations founded on the prejudices and misunderstandings of the individual. Pluralism and relativism also seems to threaten this way of thinking, because the individual is not bound by anything but a hazy notion of responsibility and his or her own values. There is clearly a danger that these values will simply be imposed on others.

Against this, however, it is worth mentioning a conviction found in many bottom-up thinkers within ethical theory, namely: that we humans have something in common that binds us together and provides a platform from which we can incarnate the ethical actions needed by the other. This commonality is typically conceived as the shared conditions of our being human: the joy of life, the fear of death, the need for love, the balancing of nature and culture, the longing for acceptance, and so on.

The strength of the bottom-up approach, as the approach has been described here, is its sensitivity to the other in concrete contexts. The problem is the risk of arbitrariness in one's interpretation of that context or situation. But one thing seems clear: a relational, situation-based ethics that emphasizes the responsibility of the individual creates a very demanding conception of what we owe others.

Key points

- Virtue ethics focuses on character or the agent, and on how he or she ought to be, rather than directly on right action. The three main components of virtue ethics are the virtues, happiness, and practical wisdom.

- A virtue is best understood as a character trait, guiding the person's actions, thoughts, preferences, habits, and so on. A person with the virtue of courage will act courageously in relevant circumstances. Happiness is probably best thought of as flourishing, and the latter is a moralized notion of what it is to live a good life in accordance with the right (wise) display of the virtues. Practical wisdom is the ability to assess how a virtue is to be exercised in a specific context: excessive courage, for example, is not genuine courage, but foolhardiness.

- It is contentious whether virtue ethics provides a "criterion of rightness", i.e. a guide to conduct capable of telling the agent, or an observer of the agent, whether a proposed course of action is morally right: *why* are the virtues *morally* good, and why is it *right* to act like a truly virtuous person?

- While many are attracted to virtue ethics, there are also many who believe that a theory of the virtues is best seen as a supplement to other ethical theories. The thought is that virtue is an interesting phenomenon in its own right, but that a comprehensive theory of ethics cannot be erected on it.

- The ethics of responsibility or situational ethics shares many traits with virtue ethics, but can nevertheless be distinguished by its focus on the ethical demand originating from the other person. The ethical demand is a demand to take care of that part of the other person's life that one has in one's hand. This should be done in an interpretation of the context and keep the interests of the other as sole goal of the action.

References

Hegel, Georg W.F. (1991): *The Encyclopedia Logic* (translated by T.F. Geraets, W.A. Suchting & H.S. Harris). Indianapolis IN: Hackett Publishing Company.

Hursthouse, Rosalind (2012): Virtue Ethics. In: Edward N. Zalta (ed.) *Stanford Encyclopedia of Philosophy (Spring 2012 Edition).* http://plato.stanford.edu/archives/spr2012/entries/ethics-virtue/

Jonas, Hans (1984): *The Imperative of Responsibility: In Search of an Ethics for the Technological Age.* Chicago IL & London: University of Chicago Press.

Levinas, Immanuel (1991): *Totality and infinity: An Essay on Exteriority.* Dordrecht: Kluwer Academic Publishers. [First published in French 1961]

Løgstrup, K.E. (1991): *Den etiske fordring* (2nd ed.). København: Gyldendal. [First published 1956] English edition: Løgstrup, Knud Ejler (1997): *The Ethical Demand.* Notre Dame IN: University of Notre Dame Press.

Further reading

Darwall, Stephen (ed.) (2002): *Virtue Ethics.* Oxford: Blackwell.

MacIntyre, Alasdair (1984): *After Virtue: A Study in Moral Theory,* (2nd ed.). Notre Dame IN: University of Notre Dame Press.

Tännsjö, Torbjörn (2002): Virtue Ethics. In: T. Tännsjö: *Understanding Ethics: An Introduction to Moral Theory,* pp. 91-105. Edinburgh: Edinburgh University Press.

Part III

The Fair

9
Equality

In parts I and II of this book we have examined theories of the good and theories of what makes an action morally right, respectively. In discussing the latter, we focused somewhat narrowly on situations in which a single agent is deliberating about what he or she should do, and in which the agent's decision affects one or two people – for example, enjoying a night out on the town or helping a friend in need. We also pursued questions about animals and the biosphere, but the primary point of this was to ask whether these cases fall within the moral circle.

What we haven't yet addressed are questions about the ethical acceptability (or legitimacy) of collective or state interference in people's lives. This is what we plan to do in part III. We begin with equality. Most of us believe that society should be fairly organized and managed, and in particular that the state can justifiably step in to remedy unjust allocations of certain goods, including wealth. Progressive taxation, for example, bears witness to this belief, and today the huge and growing gap between "rich and poor" in some western countries – not to mention the very much larger gap between developed and developing countries – is a source of grave concern and equally grave complaint. But the concept of equality, though familiar and highly evocative, is also rather abstract and slippery. What, exactly, does it bid us to share in equally? Why does equal distribution matter? Does equality matter more than other political values, such as liberty? These are questions we will turn to now.

A vivid example will serve to introduce the ethical issue we will be considering in this chapter. Originally described by the American philosopher Thomas Nagel (1979), we have adjusted it somewhat to fit our purposes more closely. Imagine you are the parent of two children,

Lucky and Unlucky. You have some surplus money which for some reason cannot be split. You can spend it on Lucky, paying for her to attend a school for gifted children where she can pursue her special interest in astrophysics, or you can spend it on Unlucky, buying some medication that will alleviate her crippling allergies to an extent. As you have probably guessed, Lucky is better off than Unlucky at the point at which you are to make this decision. Let us stipulate that Lucky has an existing welfare score of 20 and Unlucky has a score of 5. But this is not all: it also turns out that if you spend the money on Lucky she will *benefit more* than Unlucky would if you spent it on her. Their respective welfare gains would be +10 and +3. The question becomes: what should you do?

The welfare-maximizing consequentialist, or utilitarian, will have no qualms here: you should spend the money on Lucky. After all, you will add more welfare to the world by doing so. However, most people who have considered Nagel's example feel uncomfortable with this. We should think twice before going ahead and benefitting Lucky, surely. She is *better off* than Unlucky, who is, well – unlucky.

It is probably unnecessary to add that the case of Lucky and Unlucky is atypical. It was devised quite deliberately by Nagel to entail, perversely, that the utilitarian has an unavoidable moral duty to neglect the claims of the less fortunate child. Of course, typically, diverting money or other resources with general value to the more flourishing of two parties is *sub-optimal* as concerns aggregated welfare. The wealthy businessman with a substantial income, good health, two cars and a healthy pension fund will of course be happy if you give him 100 dollars, but he won't benefit from the gift to anything like the extent that a homeless child in Latin America would. Borrowing some economic terminology, moral philosophers call this phenomenon the "law of diminishing marginal utility". This dictates that, everything else being equal, the benefit of a resource declines with each additional unit acquired. Thus, in general, the better you are already doing, the less you stand to gain from an addition to your resources – e.g. a gift of money.

Awkwardly, of course, this was not the case in Nagel's example – and this is precisely why it is a fruitful case to reflect on. The example seems to show that, from an ethical perspective at least, we care about things other than maximizing total welfare. Recognizing this, most writers today have concluded that maximizing welfare cannot be our sole aim. Justice requires more than that. But if that is so, what is the more complex aim?

Three kinds of response open up at this point. The first – fuelled by examples like Nagel's, as we have seen – involves the idea that justice requires *equality* of some kind. It is not enough that the good things in life are protected, added to, or even maximized. They must also be distributed fairly in egalitarian terms. The second diagnoses the problem in the Lucky-Unlucky case rather differently. The problem is not that Lucky and Unlucky should have the same level of welfare. It is simply that, in general, we should seek to *benefit the least well off* – in this case, obviously, Unlucky. The third reaction to the maximizer's simplistic preoccupation with total welfare is again rather different. Some writers, emphasizing ownership rights and the concept of desert, stress that goods in society should be allocated to those who deserve them. If the utilitarian aim of maximizing, or the ideal of equality, or the principle that we should divert benefits to the least well off entail moving goods and resources away from people who have earned them, they condone injustice. We shall look at all of these developments in detail in what follows.

Welfare and levelling down

Egalitarians assert that equality is valuable in itself. It should be promoted and maintained for its own sake. At first sight this certainly seems to be quite a plausible view, but as we shall see in this section and the next, it is vulnerable to a range of objections. At any rate, the welfare egalitarian claims that equality of *welfare* is all we need to consider when making judgements of distributive justice. The more equal an outcome, in terms of welfare, the better, and a morally ideal outcome is achieved when well-being is distributed entirely equally.

Welfare egalitarianism is in some ways the most basic, conceptually simple position on equality. However, there are many egalitarian alternatives to it. On one view we should all have the same *resources* (e.g. the same income). On another – now a familiar tool in the political lexicon – we should all have the same *opportunities* (as in the mantra "equal opportunities for all"). A third, more minimalistic conception, says that we all have the same *rights* (for example, the hallowed principle that we all enjoy "equality before the law").

All of this serves as a valuable reminder that the term "egalitarianism" is both contentious and liable to create confusion unless it is handled carefully. Bearing this in mind, let us consider how welfare egalitarianism handles the case of Lucky and Unlucky. Welfare egalitarians, recall, hold that welfare equality is the *only* factor determining distributive justice. They would therefore be in favour of spending the money on Unlucky, simply because that will lessen the welfare inequality between Lucky and Unlucky. Spending the money on Lucky will result in welfare scores of 30 and 5 for Lucky and Unlucky, respectively. Spending the money on Unlucky will result in scores of 20 and 8 – it will mitigate, without annulling, the inequality.

How credible is the welfare egalitarian's approach here? Some might say, pretty credible. After all, the idea that we ought to benefit Unlucky is far from eccentric, and welfare egalitarianism explains why. It provides a rationale for benefitting Unlucky rather than Lucky. In actual fact, however, few moral theorists today would regard welfare egalitarianism as a plausible view. To see why, we need to look at some of the less intuitive implications of this kind of equality.

In 1997, in a famous paper, *Equality and Priority*, the Oxford philosopher Derek Parfit identified one very unappealing feature of this kind of extreme egalitarianism. Parfit asked us to imagine a world in which half the population is blind and the other half can see perfectly. A safe, successful method of transplanting one eye from a seeing person to a blind person, so they both end up with one good eye, is available. Of course this will impair the eyesight of the donor, but donors will still be able to see and function almost as before, so for most donors the reduction in welfare resulting from the loss of one eye will be marginal. The blind, however, stand to benefit *hugely* from optical transplants, so the net increase in total welfare, following surgery, will be tremendous. Many would agree that we ought to transplant eyes from the sighted to the blind. Cost-benefit calculations support this view, of course, but notice also that, as well as bringing about a net increase in welfare, the transplants would substantially improve *equality*.

So far, the welfare-maximizing consequentialist and the welfare egalitarian have no cause to disagree. But imagine a slightly adjusted case in which there is no method of transplanting eyes from the sighted to the blind. Here we cannot benefit the blind by taking one eye from each of the sighted. There is a way to improve *equality*, however: namely, by blinding all the sighted! If we do this we will achieve perfect optical equality – although no one benefits, since the sighted are now blind, whilst blind are still blind. At this point one can put a tough question to the welfare egalitarian: if *no one benefits*, why on earth should we aim for equality? Unless we can point to at least one respect in which it is better to bring about an equal distribution – that is, unless the shift to that distribution *benefits* someone – it is indeed hard to see why we should aim for equality.

The general process of attaining equality by making better off people less well-off while benefitting no one is referred to nowadays as "levelling down". Many philosophers take Parfit's levelling down case to show that welfare equality is a mistaken ideal. Parfit's case, in other words, forces us to focus on the notion that welfare equality per se is valuable, and then leaves us with little choice but to jettison that notion.

Another solution: the difference principle

Where does this leave equality? Most people believe that equality is valuable and needs to be considered in moral judgment. If welfare equality is not an option, how can we accommodate this belief without falling foul of the levelling down objection?

An influential alternative to welfarist egalitarianism was presented by the American political philosopher John Rawls (1921–2002) in *A Theory of Justice* in 1971. We say influential, but this is an understatement. Try looking at the index of just about any book on political philosophy written over the last 40 years, under the entry "Rawls". We assure you will not be disappointed. Anyway, to be precise Rawls presented his theory of justice as a response to, and rebuttal of both welfarist egalitarianism and utilitarianism. He claimed that utilitarianism fails to respect people in the right way, arguing that one individual should not be made subject to another's will to fulfil the latter's needs. Rawls asserted that we are all distinct and sovereign moral individuals who should be respected as such. If this reminds you of our earlier discussion of the ethics of rights, you are thinking along the right lines. Rawls' theory does indeed have deep roots in Kantianism. In post-Kantian political theory the notion that people have rights is central. In differing ways, the welfarist egalitarian (who is captivated by the abstract ideal of evenly spread welfare) and the utilitarian (who is similarly fixated on the abstract ideal of maximum welfare) infringe these rights by treating us all as means, or instruments, for the manipulation of welfare.

At the core of Rawls' positive proposal lies a principle of distributive justice that is best thought of as a replacement for the principle of equality. Rawls calls it the "difference principle" (DP). We shall state it in a rough and ready way, without going into the details of the goods it applies to.

DP: *Inequalities are acceptable, or just, only if they benefit the worst off.*

Let us look a bit more closely at what this means. Rawls' key insight is actually quite simple: society should be organized and managed in such a way that those who are least well off – those at the bottom of the pile – are as well off as possible. In some situations equality of welfare will ensure that the least well off are as well off as possible. Thus if five of us are asked to distribute five apples among ourselves, anything other than equal shares – one apple each – will mean that someone is doing less well than they would if the apples were shared equally. However, in other situations, equality of welfare will merely ensure that everyone is less well off than the least well off could have been given an unequal distribution of welfare.

An example will help to make this second kind of scenario more vivid. Apologists for free-market economics and the deregulation of commerce often claim that disparities in wealth are an incentive for people to work harder with greater ambition and will lead to the creation of more wealth. They are distrustful of state-imposed equality, which they take to disincentivize people, leading ultimately to the generation of less wealth. It is an article of faith for many of those with this outlook that in a free-market economy with income differentials wealth "trickles down" to the least well off. This means that disparities in wealth actually ensure that those on the lowest incomes do better than they would in an economy in which equality is imposed.

This defence of capitalism will no doubt be familiar – and, of course, you may or may not be persuaded by it. Let us assume, though, that it is broadly accurate. If we now apply DP we can see that, on Rawls' theory of justice, free-market inequality is acceptable, i.e. compatible with distributive justice. *Ex hypothesi* the inequalities of wealth here make the least well off better off than they would be if the free market was fettered and regulated with the aim of safeguarding equality.

By now the intuitive attraction of DP ought to be much clearer. In cases where inequality would benefit the least well off a dilemma arises. If they are asked "What is the *point* of equality? *Why* do you cherish it?" egalitarians appear to have two options. A natural first reply is that equality is important because it "shares goods out" and therefore benefits the poorest in society. Equality is a bit like charity in this regard. Don't we share things in primary school to make sure that the most timid child isn't left out? But the Rawlsian response to this can be readily envisaged. The Rawlsian will say: "if it is the plight of the least well off that you are worried about, your motives are laudable. In fact, as Rawlsian I share them. But you have overlooked an empirical fact: in general there is no guarantee that equality is the most effective way to improve the lot of the poorest. Sometimes equal shares benefit those who would do worse in other forms of distribution (as in the simple case of the apples mentioned above). Sometimes, however, they do not. My claim is simply that, where inequalities benefit the least well off, they are just. If you care about those with the least, you must surely agree!"

Egalitarians might now try a second kind of reply – a more properly egalitarian one. They might insist that equality is valuable in itself. However, the response to this is also easily imagined. Why on earth would *anyone* – rich or poor – want equality if it ensures merely that everyone is less well off than the poorest would be in an alternative arrangement accommodating inequality? To lobby for equality when it makes us all worse off is to fetishize an abstract ideal. (As we shall see at the end of this section, this warning against fetishizing an ideal may return to haunt the Rawlsian.)

That is the intuitive case, then. In addition to it, two important technical arguments for DP have also been pressed into service by Rawlsians. The first is contractarian in nature. Briefly, Rawls asks you, the reader, to imagine a hypothetical situation in which you are assessing principles of justice with the aim of settling on the principle, or principles, to be applied to others and you. This he calls "the original position". The key thing about the original position is that, when you are in it, you are behind what Rawls calls "a veil of ignorance". You don't know what abilities, preferences, and position you will have when the veil is lifted and you begin to tackle life in the real world. Rawls claims that in this predicament you will adopt a "maximin" strategy. You don't know what position in society you will have when the veil is drawn back. Given this, it is rational to hedge against worst-case scenarios (in which, presumably, you will discover that you have a life flipping burgers at McDonalds ahead of you, or something worse). You should seek to *max*imize *min*imal levels of welfare enjoyed in society. Doing this, you will settle on DP.

The second technical argument for DP needs a bit of introducing. We mentioned at the start of this chapter that some critics of egalitarianism are content for goods, and in particular wealth, to be distributed unequally as long as those with more have earned it and hence *deserve* their superior wealth – their fast cars, swimming pools, and costly holidays. This can be stated more formally by saying that on some theories of distributive justice deserved inequalities are legitimate.

The general idea that the distribution of benefits and burdens in society should track desert is both popular today and ancient. Many people would unhesitatingly agree that we are perfectly entitled to keep whatever we have "earned", and that "merit" should be rewarded. In doing so they would be expressing a belief Aristotle (384–322 BC) also appears to have held. *Suum cuique tribuere*, as the Ciceronian motto has it: render every man his due. Clearly, desert theories threaten to undermine simple welfare egalitarianism for the very obvious reason that the bases, or sources, of desert are not spread across the population evenly. It is an undeniable fact that some of us have more, in the way of talent and ability, than others do. Hence if it is legitimate to reward these advantages, goods will end up being distributed unevenly as well. But more importantly, for the Rawlsian, desert-sensitive theories of distributive justice also jeopardize the difference principle. They do so for similar reasons. Rawls insists that goods should be distributed so that the least well off do as well as possible. Desert theory says that goods are legitimately allocated according to talent, skill, or whatever basis of desert is agreed. It is formally possible for the outcome of these principles of distribution to coincide, but almost certainly this won't happen, and in any case as *concepts* of justice they are poles apart. For this reason Rawls needs to argue that, as a criterion of just distribution, the concept of desert is flawed.

The argument Rawls present to meet this need is what we have called the second technical argument for DP. In fact this label is misleading: the argument is no more *for* DP than it is *for* simple welfare egalitarianism, since if either of these theories is to be established the desert-based approach to justice must be disarmed. However, with this important proviso we can move on to evaluate the argument itself.

The argument runs like this. Quite what each of us deserves in goods will always depend on our talents and abilities. If you have greater talents and ability than me, you will deserve more than me of whatever is being distributed according to desert. But I have a complaint: you didn't *earn* your talents and abilities. In fact, your talents and abilities were bestowed on you by heredity, your upbringing, and more generally your environment. These factors converged very largely by luck. You had little say in them, and you certainly don't possess them deservedly. But if you don't deserve your talents and abilities, how can you be said to deserve the fruits of them? It is no good saying that you developed your talents through your own effort. People often say this, but the fact is that your ability to make that effort – which is basically a predisposition of character – is also an unearned gift you were lucky enough to be given in the natural lottery. As Rawls says:

> It seems to be one of the fixed points of our considered judgments that no one deserves his place in the distribution of native endowments, any more than one deserves one's initial starting place in society. The assertion that a man deserves the superior character that enables him to make the effort to cultivate his abilities is equally problematic; for his character depends in large part upon fortunate family and social circumstances for which he can claim no credit. (Rawls 1971, p. 104)

The upshot of this, to complete this Rawlsian attack, is that any theory of distributive justice that allocates goods on the basis of desert will distribute goods *arbitrarily* from a moral point of view. It need hardly be added that, with this defect, the desert-based theory of justice collapses. An interesting comparison can be made here between desert and rights. Desert fails as the basis of a distributive criterion because it seems to require us to have characteristics – talents, abilities and the like – whose acquisition was not just an accident of where, and when, and to whom, we were born. The Rawlsian objection, in a nutshell, is that we simply don't have characteristics like this. Drill down as far as you like, and all you will find is further accidents of character and ability. Rights, on the other hand, are very often attributed on the back of features we just happen to have, and this is completely unproblematic. Think of women's rights, children's rights and gay rights. No one would attack these on the basis that the individuals involved just happen to be women, children or gay. It would be insane to object to animal rights on the grounds that animals just *are* animals – they don't earn their animal nature!

In the 1970s the publication of Rawls' ideas reinvigorated political philosophy, and both of the technical arguments we have just set out have received considerable scholarly attention since then. It is probably fair to suggest that the second argument swam very much *with* the tide of opinion. On various grounds, many of the contemporary moral philosophers referred to in this book so far – including Ronald Dworkin, Thomas Nagel and Derek Parfit, in addition to Rawls – have queried either the coherence or the ethical significance of desert. It is worth noting, however, that in philosophical exchanges over personal morality, freedom of the will, and the justification of punishment, the notion of personal responsibility is alive and well. The consensus, if there is one, is that the concept of desert crumbles upon close examination primarily concerns distributive justice.

Rawls' argument for DP deploying the original position is more controversial. In principle it is vulnerable to criticism on two flanks. First, it might be questioned whether the original position Rawls describes is suited to the role he gives it. Can a device like the original position really be used to show what the principles of distributive justice are? Why should we care what individuals, negotiating such principles in ignorance of their own talents and abilities, agree to? Is it possible that the original position, as Rawls describes it, is merely an elaborate mechanism designed to generate the very principles Rawls and his followers find plausible to begin with? Second, even if we accept that a device like the original position is effective in revealing principles of justice, and even if we adopt the specific conditions Rawls build into this device, such as the veil of ignorance, is it absolutely clear that DP follows? Rawls claims that in the original position it would be rational to embrace a maximin strategy, and that this would lead to DP. However, is it safe to assume that the negotiators would play it safe? Is it possible that they would be less risk-averse and take a chance on an alternative to DP that is potentially more rewarding?

In a book of this nature we cannot go into the issues any further. However, we hope these questions indicate where some of the main challenges to Rawls' celebrated theory of distributive justice lie. But before we move on we must pick up a thread we left dangling some pages back. In the end, DP ranks states of affairs solely in accordance with the welfare of the least well off. You look how well the least well off are doing, and if there is an alternative arrangement under which they could be doing better, you rank that arrangement more highly. But this means that DP would rank a state of affairs in which I score 1, and everyone else scores 50, as *no better* than a state of affairs in which I score 1, and everyone else scores 2. Worse, the DP seems to imply that if I score 1 and everyone else scores 50, but there is an arrangement under which I could score 1.1 although sadly this would entail everyone else dropping down to a meagre 2, the second arrangement is preferable – indeed required by justice. Examples like these might suggest that the Rawlsian is focusing too much on the least well off. Is this a case of fetishizing an ideal?

The priority principle

So far we have examined the strengths and weaknesses of three accounts of equality. We have moved from utilitarianism, which essentially ignores distribution and hence is in conflict with our intuition that who gets what is somehow ethically important; to welfare egalitarianism, which says that an equal distribution is all that counts and is therefore unable to deal with the unpalatable phenomenon of levelling down; to the difference principle, which says that we ought to arrange distributions so as maximize the welfare of the worst off and hence fails to accommodate ideas about desert that many of us unhesitatingly subscribe to. It is high time we moved on and looked at a theory which is claimed by its supporters to resolve key problems faced by the utilitarian, the simple welfare egalitarian, and to improve on the Rawlsian DP: *prioritarianism*.

Prioritarianism is the view that benefits to the worse off are *more valuable* than benefits to the better off. If you are lucky enough to enjoy a high level of well-being, while I have a low level, my acquisition of a further 2 units of well-being, say, will be more valuable than your acquisition of the same amount. The contrast in value here is relative, not absolute. The position is not that a unit of my well-being is worth more than *any* amount of your well-being. It is rather that "pound for pound", my well-being is worth more. Hence, a sufficiently large quantity of your well-being will be worth more than a smaller quantity of mine. The valuational structure here is not unlike the pricing structure of a precious metal. Ounce for ounce, 24 carat gold has a greater monetary value than 9 carat gold, but a sufficiently large quantity of the latter will command a higher price than a smaller quantity of the former.

In effect, prioritarianism is a modified form of utilitarianism. Like utilitarians, prioritarians believe that we should distribute goods so as to maximize value, or the good. However, because they also believe that the value of additional well-being and the quantity of existing well-being are inversely related, they regard benefitting the less well off as the most effective means of maximizing – not always or necessarily, but certainly where marked inequality exists. Unlike utilitarians, prioritarians do, in this sense, "care who benefits" from maximization. They give priority to the less well off.

The following case can hopefully help to clarify the position: Abe is very badly off, but Betty is even worse off. They are both unwell. Let us stipulate that Abe has a welfare index of 3 and Betty 1. Since the average person has an index of 50, both Abe and Betty are considerably worse off than average, then. We have some medicine, but only enough for one person, so we can give it either to Abe or to Betty. Either way, the medicine will deliver a modest welfare increase of 1. Prioritarianism says we should give the medicine to Betty. Because she is even worse off than Abe, her additional unit of welfare will be worth more than Abe's – and remember, we are seeking to maximize value. In the circumstances, Betty has the highest priority.

Prioritarianism needs to be carefully distinguished from the "law of diminishing marginal utility" mentioned at the start of this chapter. The latter is sometimes invoked by utilitarians in an effort to explain why the less well-off would do well under a simple maximization strategy. Very roughly, diminishing marginal utility implies that the more a person has of something, the less he or she is able to benefit from the acquisition of more of it. A wealthy banker would benefit very little from a donation of 10 dollars. A homeless child in Latin America will benefit much more. Given this, we would almost certainly be maximizing welfare by giving the 10 dollars to the child. The prioritarian, however, believes that even if the banker is for some reason very good at converting money into welfare, and even if, as a result, he and the child stand to benefit equally from the 10 dollars, the money should go to the child. Quite simply, benefits to the worse off *matter more* than benefits to the better off. And because the child is less well off, his additional welfare is more valuable: it is like 24 carat gold as against (the banker's) 9 carat gold.

Let us turn briefly to the levelling-down objection to egalitarianism. The welfare egalitarian faces this problem because we can imagine circumstances in which the only way to achieve equality is by bringing everyone's welfare down to the level of the worst off. Plainly, this is not a very inviting proposal unless you happen to be one of the worst off and hideously envious of those with more than you. Welfare egalitarianism runs into this difficulty because it values equality in and of itself. However, prioritarianism does not ascribe intrinsic value to equality. It is maximizing theory, and it is impossible to maximize by levelling down. So, like the utilitarian, prioritarians can deal with the levelling-down objection.

Finally, like Rawls, the prioritarian needs to reject the view that welfare should be distributed in accordance with desert, since obviously value maximization is incompatible with desert theory. However, as was mentioned above, the general tide of opinion in political theory over recent years has been away from desert theories anyway. The *advantage* the prioritarian can claim over DP is this. DP, as we pointed out at the end of the last section, is obliged to rank a state of affairs in which I score 1, and everyone else scores 50, as no better than a state of affairs in which I score 1, and everyone else scores 2. It also seems to imply that if I score 1 and everyone else scores 50, but there is an arrangement under which I would score 1.1 but everyone else would get a meagre 2, the second arrangement is preferable. Basically, the Rawlsian appears to be focusing too much on the least well off. The prioritarian is in a position to respond to this worry. Everything depends on the weighting involved here. If the prioritarian assigns only a *slightly* greater value to my welfare because I am the least well off, it does not follow that [me = 1 + others = 50] is no better than [me = 1 + others = 2]. Nor does it follow that [me = 1.1 + others = 2] is preferable to [me = 1 + others = 50]. That is, on a modest differential weighting, large amounts of the less valuable welfare enjoyed by those who are well off will still add up to enough to prevent the crazy-looking Rawlsian conclusions having to be drawn. This certainly looks like an improvement on DP.

Weighting raises an obvious question about how *much* priority should be given to the worse off. If the priority is set too high, with the welfare of the worst off being accorded much greater weight, or value, than the welfare of the better off, prioritarianism becomes nearly impossible to distinguish in practice from DP: huge amounts of welfare among the better off would have to be in play to draw the focus away from the plight of the worst off. Then again, if the priority is set too low, with the welfare of the worst off being accorded only slightly greater weight, or value, than the welfare of the better off, prioritarianism becomes indistinguishable from utilitarianism: it will maximize without meaningful sensitivity to the demands of those doing least well.

The doctrine of sufficiency

In this, the final section of the chapter, we want to look briefly at a somewhat different approach to distributive justice. We will refer to this view as the *doctrine of sufficiency* (to avoid the tongue-twisting term "sufficientarianism"). Something like the doctrine of sufficiency probably lies behind the notion of "poverty lines" – lines, that is, demarcating the unacceptably poor from the merely badly off. The doctrine can also be seen as an attempt to get away from the notion, built into both DP and egalitarianism, that, *comparative* judgements of welfare fix distributive justice.

The doctrine of sufficiency says that what matters is not how much welfare you have compared with others, but whether you have *enough*, or sufficient, welfare. Welfare ought to be distributed so, that as many people as possible have a sufficient, or good enough, quality of life. The intuitive rationale for this position is quite compelling. Yes, serious inequality does seem to concern most people who think about it. However, our concern may be provoked not by the inequality as such, but more simply by the fact that those with least are unable to live a *decent life*. This is masked by the tendency, in discussions of distributive justice, to dwell on cases in which the well-being of the rich and poor is compared. But in actual fact, if the source of our moral disquiet here is the "gap" in well-being on show, we ought to be just as concerned about the gap between the rich and the super-rich, and we are not. It is therefore more fruitful to analyse the unacceptability in terms of the insufficiency of the quality of life enjoyed by the poor.

Sufficient for what, or against what measure, it might reasonably be asked? Various versions of the doctrine of sufficiency give different answers, but here is one: the morally important thing is to give people a reasonable chance to live a decent life. People should able to obtain the basic necessities of life (food, shelter, clothes). If they are unable to do so, the necessities ought to be provided for them. Moreover, in order to achieve the threshold of resources necessary for a decent *human* existence, as opposed to merely animal existence, individuals should be able to fulfil some of the higher human needs, including social, intellectual, spiritual goals. This would require, not only for a certain distribution of resources, as we normally understand the term, but also certain rights and opportunities. But once a person achieves a level of resources at which the *basic* needs necessary for a decent human life have been met, our responsibility to him, or her, drastically diminishes or disappears altogether.

Why is this? Why should a person's interests make a less powerful claim on us, as a society, once he or she has a sufficient level of well-being? One answer is as follows: what we owe to each other is first and

149

foremost the means necessary for a decent life. Once a person has these means, it is up to that person to make do with the allocated resources. Of course, this certainly does not rule out, and indeed is compatible with admiration for, charitable or benevolent assistance. It is just that, beyond the sufficiency threshold, we are talking about *supererogatory* redistribution – it is laudable to do so, but not required from an ethical perspective.

Problems with the doctrine of sufficiency can be indicated only briefly here. An obvious one is that of setting, or defining, the threshold of sufficiency. At what point, exactly, do people have enough? Less obviously, a family of difficulties revolves around counterintuitive results, or "paradoxes", of the sufficiency, wherever the threshold is set. Thus, to take just one example, suppose that a large number of people live absolutely wretched lives well below sufficiency. We have some resources which, if we allocate them to this group, will significantly improve their quality of live – however, *without* taking over the threshold into sufficiency. Alternatively we could use these resources to prevent a rather small number of people who live just above the sufficiency threshold from falling below it. The doctrine of sufficiency seems to imply that we should take the second option, but most of us would probably conclude that this is the wrong thing to do.

Key points

- Most of us have a powerful intuition that society should be fairly organized and managed, and in particular that government, or the state, can legitimately seek to correct or eliminate unjust allocations of certain goods, including wealth. This chapter examined this conviction: it addressed questions about, and theories of, distributive justice.

- The social ideal of equality is certainly an evocative one, and equality has been the rallying cry of revolutionaries down the ages. However, when we try to think through the issues, it becomes very unclear what – resources, welfare, rights, opportunities, – is meant to be equalized. The various theories of distributive justice can be regarded as proposals about where equality should lie.

- We described and assessed the merits of several theories: utilitarianism, simple welfare egalitarianism, Rawls' difference principle, prioritarianism, and the doctrine of sufficiency. Each has something to be said for it. All can be disputed. None of the theories looks like the last word on distributive justice.

References

Nagel, Thomas (1979): *Mortal Questions*. Cambridge UK: Cambridge University Press.

Parfit, Derek (1997): Equality and priority. *Ratio* 10 (3): 202-221.

Rawls, John (1971): *A Theory of Justice*. London: Oxford University Press.

Further reading

Barry, Brian (1989): *Theories of Justice, Vol. I. of A Treatise on Social Justice*. Berkeley & Los Angeles CA: University of California Press; London: Harvester-Wheatsheaf.

Frankfurt, Harry (1988): *The Importance of What We Care About*. Cambridge UK: Cambridge University Press.

Holtug, Nils & Lippert-Rasmussen, Kasper (eds.) (2006): *Egalitarianism: New Essays on the Nature and Value of Equality*. Oxford: Clarendon Press.

Kymlicka, Will (2002): *Contemporary Political Philosophy* (2nd edition). Oxford: Oxford University Press.

Nussbaum, Martha C. (2000): *Women and Human Development: The Capabilities Approach*. Cambridge UK: Cambridge University Press.

Swift, Adam (2006): *Political Philosophy: A Beginner's Guide for Students*. Oxford: Polity Press.

Temkin, Larry S. (1993): *Inequality*. Oxford: Oxford University Press.

Wolff, Jonathan (1996): *An Introduction to Political Philosophy*. Oxford: Oxford University Press.

10

Liberty[1]

The discussion of the previous chapter lay at the intersection between moral and political philosophy. Now, we will leap fully into the latter field. A classic and still highly relevant topic in political philosophy concerns the relationship – often tumultuous – between liberty and equality. This relationship connects the ideas presented in the previous chapter with those to be presented here. Perhaps, on reflection, you consider one of the distributive principles we have examined above to be essentially correct. If so, you must now face the undeniable fact that enforcing an ideal pattern of collective distribution almost always involves restricting the liberty, or freedom, of some citizens. If, for instance, the difference principle is implemented, the liberty of the talented and hardworking, and the purely lucky, to press their advantages into the service of personal gain will inevitably be curtailed. When it is applied, the difference principle intervenes and redistributes wealth from those who would obtain it through their talent or luck to those who would miss out on it because they have neither talent nor good fortune. However, distributive justice is not the only thing we cherish. We also cherish our liberty. And this means we need to ask what limits the ideal of liberty places on redistribution. Is justice without freedom real justice?

Ethical perspectives inform and guide personal decision-making. As we all know, human frailty sometimes means that we fail to live up to our own sincerely held moral beliefs, but in general, if you are a utilitarian some of your decisions will *be* utilitarian. You might, for instance, join an NGO or charity organization to help relieve poverty in the developing world. That would create more well-being than working for IBM, you think. (Possibly – it is hard to know.) If you are a Kantian,

---

[1] Many of the thoughts and arguments in this chapter are expressed brilliantly in the chapter "Liberty" in Swift (2006).

you might solemnly resolve not to lie to others on the grounds that lies are incompatible with the respect you owe to people. And so on.

Clearly, then, your ethical perspective affects *you*. It shapes your conduct. But, equally clearly, it affects *other* people. Your decision to join the NGO will make little sense if it fails to change the lives of at least some people in the developing world. It is also bound to affect the person who did take the job at IBM – the guy who, while you toil away on an irrigation system, is now working to ensure that teenage boys with a passion for computers really enjoy their lives! And naturally it affects those nearer to you, on whom you no longer spend as much time and money.

We take it that this observation needs no further emphasis. Most of us would readily agree, in fact, that moral principles are utterly pointless if they don't guide decisions that affect others. It is just as evident that, in the *political* sphere, legislation and policies implemented by the state affect pretty much everyone. Indeed they are typically designed to apply to all. Law making and policy making are driven by many factors, of course. In a democracy the need to be re-elected is a significant – some would say, too significant – consideration. But many other factors, especially economic and broadly ethical ones, exert pressure too. And among the ethical considerations politicians are obliged to reckon with we find *liberty*.

Many people care deeply about liberty. They deplore the lack of freedom endured by others in countries with draconian laws or massive social pressure to confined, predefined roles (e.g. as concerns gender), and would need to be presented with very good reasons before agreeing to give up their existing freedoms. This being so, democratically elected politicians also care about our freedom. But more than cynical electioneering is involved here. Political parties and traditions can be identified and distinguished in terms of their attitudes to liberty. We have all listened to laws and regulations being dismissed by political commentators on the right as "red tape" that stifles free enterprise. Just as often, those on the left tell us how important it is to "set free", or liberate, the talents and skills of people denied opportunities by the ruling elite. These pleas in the cause of liberty are obviously sincere. They are defining elements of the political ideologies they articulate.

Like equality, liberty (or freedom: we will use the terms interchangeably) is a central, but highly controversial, concept in political philosophy. And as with equality, it raises two main issues. The first is one of *definition*, or characterization. What exactly is liberty? What is it to exercise it, and under what conditions it is curtailed, or denied? Are there different varieties of it? We will discuss one of the well-known definitional issues: the alleged distinction between negative and positive liberty, in the section after the next.

The second issue concerns the *ethical importance* of liberty, and liberty's relationship with other personal and political values. It is fairly easy to see that liberty has a built-in tendency to come into conflict with other values. In fact it appears to be a peculiarly combative value, as some examples will show. First, depending on just how extensive it is, my freedom may well threaten the peace, health, or security – more generally, the welfare – of other people. To appreciate this, one need think merely about freedom to experiment with explosive devices. Second, my freedom might threaten yours, if we cross paths. I could block your access to a back lane by erecting a shed on a shared piece of land. Thus liberty can be in conflict, as it were, with itself. Third, my doing what I please may clash with the opinion that, even in people's private lives, certain standards of decency should be maintained, and with the moralistic view that society has the right to outlaw practices it deems immoral or offensive. Fourth, my freely made decisions may jeopardize my own well-being. Thus, if I choose to drive without a safety belt, I may injure or kill myself, and once more, here, it might be contended, paternalistically, that society has the right to outlaw forms of behaviour that involve an excessive risk of serious self-injury.

These are substantive ethical issues. Unfortunately we cannot discuss them all in this chapter, but we shall pick up some of them after the section on negative and positive liberty. The examples bring home the sheer complexity of liberty as a political value. Yes, we are all born free, but quite what follows is highly debatable.

Liberty and freedom of the will

Before going any further we need to pause for an important preliminary. Throughout the chapter it will be necessary to hold two philosophical topics safely apart. Our topic is the political, or social, value *liberty*. We have already indicated the sorts of question this value raises, definitional and substantive. Elsewhere in philosophy, however, on the borders of ethics and metaphysics (the study of the most general and fundamental nature of things), a better known debate rages over "freedom of the will", or free will, and responsibility.

In the briefest of summaries, the difficulty here is to explain how we could ever be said to act freely when we live in a physical world which is governed throughout by causal laws and hence, as far as we can tell, is *deterministic*. If your conduct can be traced to physical causes – such as brain activity and sensory inputs – how can you be said to act freely? Could you ever have done other than you actually do? If not, are you a free, or responsible, agent? And in any case, would an act that is somehow detached from the causal network be on that account free, or just random?

This is a fascinating area of philosophy, but in the present book we cannot go into it. We need to focus on the political issue of liberty alone. In proceeding in this way we are not suggesting that the two issues are unrelated. They most certainly are not. The point is just that it is very hard to make headway with questions about liberty while at the same time trying to think through questions about free will. The decision to set aside the latter is largely pragmatic.

Negative and positive freedoms

In a now famous lecture entitled "Two Concepts of Liberty" Isaiah Berlin (1909–1997) argued that the single term "liberty" masks a plurality of meanings (Berlin 1969, pp. 118ff). He stressed, in particular, two aspects of liberty in political philosophy. To disentangle these two fundamental senses of liberty, suppose you are a dietary vegan – you don't eat meat, or any foods produced by animals, including eggs and milk – living in a contemporary western democracy. You, the vegan, might claim to be free to only eat non-animal foods, since no one is *forcing* you not to eat non-animal foods. There are no laws which stipulate that you have to eat at least some meat (e.g. an obligatory Sunday roast), and there are no laws forbidding you from eating a vegan diet. One sense of liberty, then, seems to be *negative*. It means you are free to act in the absence of some obstacle or interfering force. You have a *freedom from* outside forces that prevent you from being vegan.

But vegans might be said to be free in a different way. Barring extreme poverty, you are free to go ahead and buy, or grow, non-animal food products. In this sense, you have the *opportunity* to go ahead and buy bean curds, if you wish. Another sense of liberty, then, seems to be *positive*: the claim that you are free in this second sense connotes the actual possibility of doing, or achieving, something. It is a *freedom to* act – to actually obtain bean curds.

Consider this example. The authors of this book might have the *negative* liberty to become professional footballers. There is no legal obstacle to them doing this – no law, for example, forbidding philosophers to play football. However, it is evident that we do not have the *positive* liberty to do this. It would require skills and physical prowess of a kind we do not possess. We are free from constraints, yet we are not free to actually become professional footballers. True, we can take limited, but much appreciated consolation, in the fact that Cristiano Ronaldo will probably not take up moral philosophy.

So we seem to have (at least) two very different senses of liberty. Both the history of philosophy and everyday discourse are full of examples of people who have considered the distinction between negative and positive freedom to be extremely important. Berlin said: "The fundamental sense of freedom is freedom from chains, from imprisonment, from enslavement by others. The rest is extension of this sense, or else metaphor" (Berlin 1969, p. lvi). He was indeed a champion of negative liberty. In crude terms this normally entails defending free markets, a limited and not too powerful state, and individual property rights of the kind that afford protection against massive redistribution. But others have sought to promote the claims of positive freedom. Again, in crude terms, this implies an emphasis on redistribution, protection against the vagaries of the market, and "positive rights" i.e. rights *to* something such as money, or education, or healthcare.

Does this twofold division of liberty stand up to close examination? It might be meaningful to describe a situation in terms of the agent's freedom from or freedom to. However, when we look closely at a specific freedom like freedom of expression, it seems that any thorough description will involve both kinds of liberty. Thus freedom of expression evidently includes negative elements (a lack of censorship, the absence of reprisals) *and* positive elements (the ability to communicate, effective access to means of communication, an audience). In fact, it seems hard to speak of any concrete freedoms that cannot always be formulated in terms *both* of freedom from and of freedom to. Your freedom to walk down the street is also a freedom from being molested when you do so. Your freedom from religious persecution is also a freedom to pursue the religious path of your choice, or to eschew religion altogether. Perhaps a more satisfying way of describing specific liberties is to say that, whenever they are real, they involve both negative and positive elements. (The reader will hopefully see that many of the issues involved here concerning negative and positive liberty mirrors the discussion of negative and positive rights in chapter 7.)

Does this mean that Berlin's distinction, and the substantive implications of it, should be ignored? No. The distinction remains a very useful way of getting a grip on the notion of freedom. Perhaps it ought to be modified somewhat, however.

Let us return to dietary veganism. Imagine that you, a vegan, live in a society where there are no laws prohibiting the sale of vegan produce. Suppose, also, that you are not only vegan: you also insist that the things you eat are organic. Unfortunately, it just so happens that you live in a town where people do not care much for organic and vegan produce.

The shops and restaurants often stock *only* animal products and non-organic vegetables.

In this situation we can describe your freedom in the following way: you have *formal* freedom to be an organic vegan. No laws prohibit this, and there are no social sanctions of the sort that would strongly deter you from that diet. But at the same time you lack *effective* freedom to be an organic vegan. Of course, you can freely choose to die of starvation, but that is hardly a relevant sense of the freedom involved.

The formal/effective distinction really does separate importantly different aspects of freedom. Often granting, or guaranteeing, formal freedom is a freebie. It simply involves ensuring that no legal or social impediments (bans, prohibitions, and the like) stand in a person's way. In contrast, securing *effective* freedom can be costly. Imagine the amount of money and time that would be necessary to turn the authors of this book into professional footballers!

The distinction between left and right in politics, unclear as it may be, sometimes maps neatly on to the formal-effective distinction – at least, as far as economics is concerned. Normally, those on the political right advocate formal freedom and those on the political left champion effective freedom.

The formal-effective distinction is not beyond criticism, however. Most obviously, it is exposed to two kinds of attack – one from the right and the other from the left. If you look closely at the idea of effective freedom, it seems to presuppose formal freedom. You might have the means (i.e. the money) to buy vegetables and other non-animal products, and somebody may be trying to sell you beetroots, but you do not really have the effective freedom to go ahead if the law forbids the sale of beetroots. Your effective freedom here appears to have limited value. But – and this is the important point – what is the *freedom* specifically involved in effective freedom, then? How does it differ from formal freedom? In the beetroot example you had the resources (the money), and you had the opportunity to purchase (someone wanted to sell you beetroots). But is it accurate or helpful to call resources and opportunities freedom? Would it not be more precise to describe them as resources and opportunities? If this is along the right lines, perhaps Berlin's "freedom from chains"-sentiment illustrates not so much the fundamental, but the *only* meaningful sense of freedom.

On the other hand, it might be insisted that formal freedom is not really freedom at all in the true sense. Imagine you have no money to buy vegetables. According to champions of formal freedom this is not the key factor determining whether you are free to be an organic vegan. The state gives you formal freedom: it has not banned the sale of vegetables. That means you are free. But if formal freedom does not actually enable you to act, in what sense is this freedom important to you? We all know that the fact that there is no formal obstacle to disadvantaged young people becoming doctors and lawyers does not show they have an equal chance of progressing in medicine or law. The state's protection of formal freedoms offers very little of real benefit.

Liberty and equality

It is hard to see how this dispute between the political left and right is going to be resolved once and for all. Perhaps we ought to say that *real* liberties almost always involve both effective and formal freedom, but that is only superficially helpful. The disagreement we have just sketched is less about what freedom *is*, and more about what freedom *merits* in the way of state protection. In effect, this brings us back to questions about the relative importance of different political values. With this in mind, let us address the relationship between liberty and other values more directly, concentrating first on equality.

Many believe that liberty should be tempered by equality, since only then can it be guaranteed that when we exercise our freedom we will not illegitimately hinder others from exercising theirs as well. Freedom should, in a sense, be *equal* freedom. Even Berlin, a staunch defender of liberty, acknowledged that freedom for the pike means death for the minnows. This does not imply that freedom and equality must be compromised if only one in two hopeful students can take up the place in medical school: both "freedom" and "equality" require interpretation, and if equality is interpreted as equal opportunity, then the two students *are* equal if they have equal opportunity to obtain the qualifications needed for medical school – assuming, of course, that no other distorting forms of discrimination lay behind the decision to pick one rather than the other student. It *does* mean, however, that in most circumstances there is an inherent potential for conflict between the ideals of liberty and equality: some ways of expanding freedom will minimize equality. You might greatly expand the range of opportunities for the most talented 75% of the population by refraining from educating the least talented 25%. A focus on educating the talented could plausibly release resources spent on educating the least talented. Conversely, equality might require us to ensure that the most talented 75% of a population have no education, thus levelling the playing field and "benefitting" the least talented 25% (see the discussion of "levelling down" in the previous chapter).

Both of those options might seem perverse, yet we will often have to steer somewhere between such extreme courses of action. When making political decisions, we are often faced with choices that have implications for freedom and equality, and very often, we cannot maximize both. Moreover, *inaction* will probably entrench existing frameworks of power, and hence their consequences for freedom and equality. So "not acting" is a choice for which we can be held politically, and hence morally, responsible. We need to face up to this challenge, and to find out which course of action is *legitimate*. Political action, or refraining from political action, is a moral choice which needs to be underpinned by valid reasons.

Equality, liberty, and the requirements of justice

The legal and political philosopher Ronald Dworkin (1931–2013) claimed that all plausible political theories stand on an egalitarian platform. We have already touched upon this issue, but briefly Dworkin's claim is not that all plausible political theories advocate equality of income, or a variant of this view such as one of the theories of redistribution we encountered in the chapter on equality. Rather his claim is that any political theory that states that some classes of citizen – say, women, blacks, homosexuals, or non-believers – are worth less than others is implausible.

Essentially, we expect the same of a political theory as we do of a moral theory: in the absence of other weighty considerations, the state owes us equal respect and concern. Some believe that it follows from this that we should aim to redistribute resources, such as income, substantially. For them, equal respect implies equal shares of income or welfare. For others, however, equal respect does not entail, nor is it so much as compatible with, redistribution. Nonetheless, equal respect remains a fundamental requisite of a plausible political theory. We will take a closer look at one such theory below.

In all the important respects, a fully worked out theory of justice must explain how the collective action of the state affects people's rightful share of resources, welfare, opportunities, or whatever else is agreed to be desirable whoever you may be. The theory ought to explain when and why the differential impact of state policies on people's share can be justified. Why is this so important? The answer is simply that we do not want the fate of the individual to be left to unjust and arbitrary circumstances. If justice means treating "like cases alike", or "giving to each his or her due", it follows that the key challenge for a theory of justice lies in explaining when an unequal impact is justified, if ever.

The Canadian political theorist Will Kymlicka has suggested that the challenge here is to reconcile two intuitive but conflicting principles. On the one hand, we want a theory of justice to "ignore" *arbitrary circumstances or endowments* (talents, capacities) that can affect people's life chances. Being born in a rich family – or a poor one – is morally arbitrary. Thus it should not have unequal impact on our lives. "Ignore" here means that the pattern of distribution across citizens that results from a theory of justice should not reflect such arbitrary circumstances. Naturally, this reflects a specific ideal of equality: we should not allow inequality that arises from arbitrary circumstances. On the other hand, we do want to hold people responsible in both a negative and positive way for their *choices*, insofar as they do not wholly reflect arbitrary circumstances. If we have two people, roughly equally well-equipped mentally and resourced, and one chooses to put all his or her efforts into a job, leaving little or no time for other pursuits, and the other chooses a lifestyle involving an undemanding job and copious spare time, we should not, from the point of view of *justice*, at any rate, have any quarrel with the result when the first person ends up having more resources than the second. Inequalities that arise from people's choices are not problematic. They might even be commendable, so the theory of justice should be choice-responsive. Naturally, this ideal reflects an affirmative evaluation of liberty: you should be free to work to improve your life, and you are not obliged to bear the burden of other people's imprudent choices.

Neat as this distinction between arbitrary circumstances or endowments and choice may seem, controversies are bound to arise. In reality the state can never be perfectly circumstance-ignorant, and achieve complete equality, whilst at the same time respecting a minimum of personal liberty. Some people are so badly off in terms of natural endowments and talents that, no matter what we do, we can never compensate them fully for their disadvantages. We could continue to transfer resources away from the talented and hardworking, or away from those who are plain lucky, and still not fully equalize their circumstances, or provide adequate compensation – unless, of course, we make *everyone* equally badly off by "levelling down", which as we saw last chapter is hardly an acceptable solution. Even limited compensation would almost certainly involve a significant reallocation of resources from the talented to the ordinary, thereby curtailing the former's liberty. On the other hand, if the liberty of talented, hardworking and lucky individuals is given greater priority, less compensation will result. This would compromise equality and restrict the effective liberty of those who are ordinary or unlucky. In short, the state can never *fully* satisfy both liberty and equality, at least not by the measure of large-scale distributive principles. Things might look differently in smaller settings and where people do not differ hugely in terms of endowment and resources. However, if we aim for an ambitious ideal of justice encompassing everyone, we are bound to find that people differ in important, yet arbitrary aspects.

From a common sense view it is necessary to find a plausible middle way between these two principles. But what is 'plausible' here will depend, to a large degree, on your conception of moral responsibility. If you think people are responsible for the vast majority of their actions, you will tend to emphasize choice-sensitiveness and, maybe, also to oppose large-scale redistribution. However, if you are sceptical about the notion of personal responsibility and believe that we are largely, or wholly, the product of random circumstances, you will probably advocate significant redistribution from the lucky and talented to the unlucky and unskilled.

This last point is a major theme in a recent addition to, or development of, Rawlsian political philosophy. So-called *luck egalitarians* champion a conception of justice where one's relative "distributional fate" should not be determined by *brute* luck. Brute luck here means the upshots of circumstances for which one is not responsible. So neither the lucky rich nor the unlucky poor deserve their relative distributional fates. However, if you *choose* to take a risk, e.g., in a lottery, and you end up losing all your money, society owes you no compensation (on ground of justice, at least.) Of course, you have been unlucky, but effects of good or bad *option* luck (as compared with *brute* luck) do not merit compensation etc.

With some effort, luck egalitarianism can be understood as a way of trying to reconcile equality and liberty: equality as concerns effects of brute luck; liberty as concerns the results of option luck, voluntary choices etc. Luck egalitarianism, then, highlights the question of *responsibility*, because it becomes of paramount importance to determine which, if any, of our actions are actions for which we are responsible. In that way, luck egalitarianism invites us into the territory concerning free will etc. that we said from the beginning we would not enter. Hence, we shall not.

Against redistribution: libertarianism

Are we assuming a little too readily that political justice is responsibility-sensitive and gives rise to claims of compensation? Can it be argued that it is not the business of the state to redistribute at all? This attitude is perhaps less outlandish than it seems. Certainly, it has been denied that justice requires the state to guarantee a "pattern" of distribution of resources and opportunities. Some would say that the fact that Abe has a low income and few opportunities, while Belinda has a high income and many opportunities, is in itself irrelevant to justice.

What is relevant is how these inequalities arose. It is the *history*, rather than the *pattern*, of distribution that is the important thing. As long as Belinda has not infringed Abe's rights by stealing from him, or cheating him, or some such thing, justice is satisfied. Inequality is not as such unjust. This means furthermore that Belinda and Abe are at liberty to pursue many projects that might lead to inequality – for as long as they do not infringe on other persons' rights.

We will now discuss two arguments for this view, both of which have emerged from the *libertarian* tradition. Most libertarians base their ethical viewpoint on a strong notion of *self-ownership*: we own ourselves, and we are furthermore responsible for our choices and the outcomes. This gives rise to important negative rights. For example, it is claimed that you are not permitted to interfere with my choices – at least, insofar I do not infringe upon *other* peoples' choices or rights. The same goes for the state. Most crucially, we have strong rights of property which severely limits coerced taxation and state-borne redistribution. The libertarian does not see this as inconsistent with equality. After all, we *all* have the same robust rights.

What might lead one to adopt this view? The leading twentieth-century libertarian Robert Nozick (1938–2002), encountered in chapter 9, once provided an influential example illustrating one line of thought behind the libertarian position (Nozick 1974, pp. 160-162). Imagine that initially everyone has the same resources. (We could imagine almost any kind of initial distribution, but let us stick with an equal distribution for now.) Enter Wilt Chamberlain, basketball star. A lot of people are willing to pay to see Wilt do his stuff, and Wilt signs a contract giving him one dollar per ticket sold throughout the season. Let us say 250,000 tickets are eventually bought by fans all of whom are happy to pay the ticket price. At the end of season, then, Wilt has 250,000 dollars. He is richer than everyone else.

Nozick's provocative question is: "what is wrong with this?" After all, the fans were free to buy tickets or not to do so. Nobody *forced* them to pay. Much the same can be said of all the other parties involved. They acted freely, without duress or coercion. In Nozick's memorable phrase, what could ever be wrong with "capitalist acts between consenting adults"?

Before we acquiesce and reply "nothing at all" let us examine more closely the situation. Clearly, if you only have a moral complaint when you are forced into a transaction, the fans have no moral complaint. Taking Wilt as our guide to justice the conclusion must be that, in the absence of some form of coercion, there is nothing wrong with someone ending up with more than others. What *would* be wrong would be forcing customers to use their money in ways to which they have not freely consented. So, if a customer has obtained money legitimately, how could it ever be legitimate for the state to tax Wilt's games? And in general how can it ever be legitimate for the state to tax people, possibly against their will, for redistributive reasons?

We will postpone critical analysis for a moment and present the second libertarian argument against the legitimacy of coerced redistribution. As we said, libertarians base their position on the notion that we own ourselves. From a moral point of view, this seems to be a reasonable starting point: who else should it be, especially if we need a robust rendering of the idea of equal respect? It is said to follow that we own our bodies and our various talents, mental or otherwise. Again, this is both reasonable and seems to accord with the dynamics of equal respect. The crucial step in libertarian thought is *from* the belief that we own ourselves *to* the claim that we own the fruits of our labour. For if that is the case, if we do indeed own the fruits of our own labour, how could we be required legitimately by the state to pay taxes to fund redistribution? Naturally you may *choose* to donate money to charity. That would be both commendable and legitimate. But, since you own yourself, you also own your income, and therefore compulsory taxation becomes a kind of theft, and theft has no part in justice.

These two arguments have been met with much criticism. Many of the objections appear ultimately to boil down to one complaint – namely, that libertarians ignore the distinction between *choice* and *circumstances* that we discussed earlier. Consider the Wilt Chamberlain example, and let us assume the distribution is equal initially. Now, are people's circumstances the same? Evidently, Wilt's are quite different from the circumstances of others. His skill at basketball is a valuable commodity he can sell on the market. If he is not entitled to take credit for his basketball skills, or is not entitled to take full credit, there is no justice in his reaping the full benefits of his talent. The libertarian may retort that we should assume everyone had the same circumstances, and that Wilt just *chose* to use his talents when others did not. This merits two replies. First, as we saw earlier, a "talent for using talents" might be an undeserved talent in itself. Second, even if everything in the example really *is* the product of free, un-coerced choice, it might still be *a bad thing* if some people have nothing and others a lot.

In the argument from self-ownership, the choice-circumstance distinction appears again, albeit this time in a less obvious manner. Libertarians and their opponents might share the same starting point – namely, that we own ourselves, but the crucial step in the libertarian train of thought is the jump from self-ownership (I own my body and talents) to property rights (therefore, I own the fruits of my labour.) Does the fact that I a) own my body and talents straightforwardly *entail* that b) I own the fruits of my labour? Many maintain that libertarians have failed to support this inference adequately. Some libertarians argue that if we are to respect a) we must uphold b). But if we want *equal* respect for a) (i.e. equal respect for the self-ownership of each and every individual), it seems that we should at least admit that each and every individual has a right to some minimal means of subsistence. This in turn could be used to argue for *some*, albeit minimal, forms of redistribution. Indeed, when pressed, quite a few libertarians argue for one or the other form of such redistribution, for instance in the form of negative income tax.

What about community?

You are doubtless familiar with the French revolutionary slogan *Liberté, Égalité, Fraternité* (or with a modern English variant substituting "community", or "solidarity", for "fraternity"). In this chapter liberty and equality have been in the foreground, but it might be said that we need to address the claims of *fraternité* as well: the concept of community as it is implicated in the concept of justice.

The last three or four decades have witnessed two major philosophical attempts to revitalize the theorization of community. First, a perspective on justice known as "communitarianism" emerged. This emphasized community, culture, social cohesion and solidarity without using socialist notions such as class or exploitation. In general, it also emphatically rejected moral universalism – the notion that at least some moral values hold true across all communities and cultures. Later "republicanism" or, as it is sometimes called, "neo-republicanism" came into vogue. This latter view has no direct connection with anti-royalism or the American Republican Party. It is less preoccupied with culture and close-knit communities than communitarianism, and it is not normally anti-universalist. Advocates of republicanism believe, however, that a "spirit of community" (a preparedness to set aside one's own interests in the name of the greater good) is valuable and necessary for justice, and that this is insufficiently acknowledged in theories of justice relying merely on the concepts of liberty and equality.

Communitarians would also endorse these last two points: they and neo-republicans both insist that community is *necessary*, and that sometimes at least, liberty and equality are required to give way to community. Here, however, it is very important to distinguish between two rather different claims. The first is that community is *instrumentally* valuable because it tends to promote the things we regard as intrinsically good, such as a political settlement in which liberty and equality are adequately respected. Thus, it is often asserted that the

165

redistributive welfare policies are crucially dependent on a widespread sense of community and solidarity. Without an established sense of community, ensuring that people are willing, at least some of the time, to identify with collective needs rather than their own alone, requisite levels of taxation simply could not be maintained. Nor, as a society, could we expect to enjoy general respect for the rule of law. The second claim, by contrast, pictures community as a goal in itself – that is, as something with *intrinsic* value.

The first claim is hard to quibble with. The gist of it – that the state would be unable to function properly in the absence of a sense of solidarity or of identification with community – is plausible, certainly. But this leaves ample room for discussion about details, and, as it were, just *how much* "community" we need, instrumentally speaking. The second claim probably has fewer admirers. It is self-evident that communities can be beneficial *and* harmful at the same time: they can benefit some of their members and be harmful to others. But if this is true, the idea that community is valuable in itself becomes unclear.

Key points

- A serious challenge, both political and philosophical in nature, is set by the tendency of liberty and equality to pull in different directions. Some political arrangements respect individual liberty to the detriment of equality, and vice versa, and there are situations in which it appears to be impossible to pursue the ideals of liberty and equality fully at the same time.

- Liberty is sometimes treated as a two-pronged concept: negative liberty (freedom *from* interference or restraint) and positive liberty (the actual ability, or freedom, *to* do what you wish to do). Real cases of liberty always seem to involve elements of both. You are not free *to* walk down the street unless you are also free *from* the efforts of a captive, for example.

- It is perhaps better to speak of *formal* and *effective* liberty. Here "formal" means roughly that there are no legal or other sanctions against you acting on a decision, and "effective" means that you are actually in a position to exploit your formal liberty.

- Equality interacts with liberty in a variety of ways. Many believe that a satisfactory theory of justice must be sensitive to the fact that the *circumstances* of citizens vary enormously. We should not hold people responsible for their circumstances, because circumstances are un-chosen and hence morally arbitrary. This perspective favours redistribution and equality, but it is often tempered by the notion that we should hold persons responsible for their *choices.*

- Libertarian theories of justice ignore patterns of distribution and focus solely on historical transactions, or the *way* in which a given distribution of goods arose. One this approach, as long as there are no moral objections to the way a distribution has come about (e.g. no one has been coerced or manipulated), there can be no moral complaint about the distribution, even if it is unequal.

- Libertarian theories of justice have been rejected by communitarians, who believe that the libertarian works with a false conception of the self and overlooks the fact that community is a good.

References

Berlin, Isaiah (1969): *Four Essays on Liberty.* Oxford: Oxford University Press.

Nozick, Robert (1974): *Anarchy, State, and Utopia.* New York: Basic Books.

Swift, Adam (2006): *Political Philosophy: a Beginners Guide for Students and Politicians.* Cambridge UK: Polity Press.

Further reading

Barry, Brian (1989): *Theories of Justice*, vol. I. of *A Treatise on Social Justice.* Berkeley & Los Angeles CA: University of California Press; London: Harvester-Wheatsheaf.

Dworkin, Ronald (1977): *Taking Rights Seriously.* London: Duckworth.

Hobbes, Thomas (several editions): *Leviathan.* [First published 1651] See e.g. http://www.publicliterature.org/books/leviathan/1

Kymlicka, Will (2002): *Contemporary Political Philosophy: An Introduction* (2nd ed.). Oxford: Oxford University Press.

Wolff, Jonathan (1996): *An Introduction to Political Philosophy.* Oxford: Oxford University Press.

11

Democracy[2]

In the western world it is widely believed that individuals ought to be able to control central aspects of their lives. We view individuals as "authors of their own life," as opposed to blind puppets of fate, chance, their class, their sex, and so forth. In other words, we value a certain form of personal autonomy. We live together in political communities – thankfully, you might say – and we therefore need rules and decision procedures in order to live together in a way which allows us to reap the fruits of cooperation and community, whilst protecting each individual's autonomy. The usual, and most popular, method of doing this is democracy. However, democracy is a contested and complex phenomenon. In this chapter, we will introduce some philosophical questions and controversies raised by democracy. We will ask whether all decisions made by a democratic majority are legitimate and whether more democracy (a wider scope for democratic decisions) is better than less? What does pluralism mean for democracy? Should we adopt a representative or direct form of democracy? What is the role of culture? Should we have a world government?

Most of our decisions affect other people. Sometimes in ways they do not want. We sometimes seek agreement with others on what to do, and when we are successful our wills and those of the people affected by our actions come into harmony. In the "private sphere" such harmony is desirable, but not generally something others can demand. It may be better if you and I can agree over the renovation or removal of the ramshackle caravan in my driveway, but I am probably not obliged to repair it or get rid of it. In the "public sphere" we tend to believe that harmony is more important: people are entitled to be consulted over

---

[2] Many of the arguments in this chapter are borrowed from the chapter "Democracy" in Swift (2006).

proposals, plans and policies, and where the consultation throws up a range of opinions we tend to try to please as many people as possible.

The political arrangement we refer to as *democracy* reflects this attitude to the public sphere. Its underlying assumption is that *unanimous* decisions are ideal, because they are not in conflict with anyone's will. But, of course, everyone recognizes that, nearly always, we shall have to settle for less. If unanimous decisions were the only sort allowed, and acted upon, we could rarely, if ever, call a decision democratically legitimate and collective decisions would be all but impossible.

When exactly is a decision democratically legitimate? The obvious, but rather unsatisfying answer is: whenever a majority is in favour of the decision in question. Decisions can be legitimate simply because they are favoured by the majority. This is true of decisions where there simply isn't a right answer in the absence of a vote. Take the question whether to drive on the left or right side of the road. There is no correct answer to this question, but everyone is much better off if we all drive on the *same* side, ensuring the safe flow of traffic. A majority vote here seems to settle the matter satisfactorily: no matter what is decided, we are all better off when we have made a decision and stick to it. However, only few questions are of this kind.

Political decisions will often leave some better off, and others worse off. If a simple majority bestowed legitimacy on a decision, it would be democratically legitimate to decide, for example, that red-haired people should pay 10% extra in tax, or not receive public healthcare, or be forced to take up certain occupations and barred from others. But from a moral point of view such decisions are arbitrary and unjustified. They are not *morally* legitimate. Moral legitimacy – or rightness – is independent (at least sometimes) of democratic legitimacy because democratic decision procedures might lead to morally unacceptable decisions and outcomes. On the other hand, in the light of the often reasonable *disagreement* about what constitutes moral rightness, we can have reasons to accept certain democratic decisions even if they do not perfectly reflect some moral ideal. In short: the relation between morality and democracy is tricky indeed.

The crucial question is therefore: in what circumstances can people be legitimately required by law, backed by sanctions, to abide by the decisions of the majority? In other words: what are the conditions of democratic legitimacy, *morally* speaking?

It helps to begin with the question: why should we submit to democracy at all – what justifies democracy? Assume that modern states owe each of their citizens some sort of fundamental respect. Treating people with respect normally involves treating them as competent and autonomous individuals who are able to control their own affairs and lives, at least within certain limits. Every competent adult should be able to exercise a degree of control over the part of the world he or she inhabits. Since the state regulates the affairs of the people, this idea seems to imply that citizens should be allowed a say in affairs of state: they are entitled to participate in public debate, vote for representatives, or vote directly on important political decisions, to lobby for their favoured political candidate or cause, or to run for office themselves, and so on.

Naturally, controversy is bound to arise because citizens have different ideals, goals and values. Here is one example: One faction in society might believe that people ought to be held responsible for their own lifestyle choices. While such people might respect an individual's freedom to smoke and drink heavily, they may also want to hold them responsible for such choices, and hence they may believe that society should not foot the bill if smokers and drinkers fall prey to lifestyle-related diseases such as lung cancer, diabetes or cirrhosis of the liver. Another faction might insist that holding people responsible for a disease that is a result of their lifestyle is callous, or the result of flawed reasoning. How should society, or rather the state, handle such conflicts, whilst upholding the ideal that the democratic state ought to respect every citizen, and that all competent adults should be allowed to exercise a degree of control over their own affairs?

The question how the powers of the state can be used legitimately – in law, regulation, taxation, welfare provision, the healthcare system, and so on – is a central theme here. Another theme is the specific condition in which these powers are exercised: the fact of *pluralism*. Here, "pluralism" refers to the fact that citizens in modern societies espouse a plurality of world-views, conceptions of the good (ideas about what makes their lives go well), lifestyles, religious points of view, moral ideals, and more generally preferences. Pluralism does not automatically lead to conflict – even profound moral and religious discrepancies do not automatically tear societies asunder or lead to inter-group alienation. But in a plural society there is inherently, and necessarily, potential for conflict.

This reframes the basic political philosophical question about legitimacy. This question now becomes: if we want democratic decisions (and the state as such) to be legitimate, *how should we arrange our political institutions given the fact of pluralism*? After all, given the obvious multiplicity of beliefs about issues such as social justice, religion, science, the environment, sexual orientation, and so forth, it seems inevitable that one of the main purposes of the modern state must be to *accommodate* plurality. As far as possible the state must

171

sustain reasonably peaceful co-existence between the different groups and subgroups in society whilst respecting every citizen. But how is this to be done?

Democracy

In the nineteenth century Abraham Lincoln (1809–1865) described democracy as *"government of the people, by the people, for the people"*. This is probably very close to the best interpretation of the *concept* of democracy. The slogan expresses fundamental features every democratic state must possess to some degree. Of course, democracy is government *of* the people, since all state government is. There need be no disagreement between democrats and their opponents on this matter. Nevertheless, it is still a highly controversial theme, for *who* are "the people"? If the idea is that competent adults should have a say in affairs affecting them, shouldn't we be trying to clarify *global* democracy? Many decisions made by the governments of USA or China affect people in the rest of the world, after all. We shall return to this question later. For the time being we will proceed on the basis that we are dealing with democracy of the nation state.

Lincoln's "by the people" must mean that all relevant persons in the political community have a say, whilst "for the people" must mean that the government is for the *benefit* of the people and not some economic or religious elite, or for the sake of an ideal that is detrimental to the interests of the people. As you can probably see, although "democracy" has a definitional core, there is scope for substantive disagreement. There is agreement, more or less, on the *concept* of democracy, but there is no agreement on the best *conception* of democracy: how should we, when we go into details, flesh out that conception?

Among the most pressing issues is the question of the *scope* of democratic decisions: how (if at all) and why should we *limit* democratic decision-making so as to exclude democratically legitimate yet morally objectionable decisions? Or can a democratic majority justify just *any* decision?

It is useful to think of the positions on this question as falling along a spectrum, with anarchism at one extreme and totalitarianism at the other. Anarchists believe that *no* decisions should be enforced by a state. For them there are *no* democratically legitimate decisions, and so the scope for democratic decision-making is zero. The unlimited democrat believes that in principle *any* kind of decision is suitable for democracy. The scope for democracy is unlimited. Whereas the first extreme makes the state impossible, it can plausibly be argued that the second extreme is more *democratic*. But the second extreme is not better because of this.

If this sounds odd, that is because the term "democracy" has positive connotations. But consider for a moment whether it really would be a good thing if, in principle, everything could be decided by a democratic vote: there would be no principled protection of minorities, no protection of privacy, no fundamental rights to protect individuals against majority democratic decisions. A democratic decision could overrule any kind of individual decision. For instance, your choice of partner, or whether you should drink milk or water, or the length of your hair, could be questions to be decided by majority vote. If you accept such considerations as morally relevant, you will agree that we cannot say that some state of affairs x is better than some state of affairs y simply in virtue of x being "more democratic."

To cut a long story short: it is generally agreed that democracy must be tempered and constrained by protection for vulnerable minorities from electoral majorities and protection of the individual's rights. The real question is not whether democracy should be unlimited, but rather how broad the scope of democracy ought to be. To answer this we need to take a brief detour into moral epistemology – that is, the study of how, if at all, we know whether something is morally right or wrong.

Some decisions would not be "right" in any sense of the word in the absence of a democratic mandate. We have already noticed this with the example of whether we should drive on the left or right of the road. There is no independent truth of the matter before we make the decision. It is, as we might say, democracy-dependent. Such cases are uncontroversial. Democracy is as fine a method for making decisions in them as any other.

However, other matters are far more controversial. Let us return to the division of those who believe we should be held responsible for our lifestyle choices and those who believe we should not. What is the truth of this matter? Is there an *independent* truth? Does it cover all individuals, or is the truth subjective, such as to change from person to person? The truth might depend on a democratic decision. However, the wisest course of action is perhaps *not* to decide on the matter democratically, but rather to allow people decide for themselves. However, does *not* deciding on the matter imply subsidizing people with unhealthy lifestyles, or not? If there is a collective, tax-based insurance system in place, and this pays for everyone's healthcare, then, in certain circumstances, those who make healthy lifestyle choices could end up subsidizing those with unhealthy lifestyles. However, this seems unfair, unless we can say that we are not responsible, or sufficiently responsible, for our lifestyles. But unfortunately this is exactly the question which is in dispute. It seems that no matter what decision we end up with (or if we abstain from taking a decision), we are going to

173

force a moral view on some part of the electorate that they do not accept.

Politics is often called "the art of the possible". At least two interpretations have been offered, both of which stress that the art of politics takes place within a democratic framework and under conditions of pluralism. First, there is a pragmatic and moderate interpretation: given that potential and real conflicts of interest are inherent in pluralistic societies, we have to emphasize stability, compromise and consensus. We need to strike deals constantly between conflicting sectors of the populace. We cannot allow one sector to have the upper hand in all decisions, which would lead to widespread dissatisfaction and possible civil unrest. In short, democracy implies a moderate, peaceful way of making decisions. This might be true – or at least prudent. However, the drawback of this response to pluralism is that it does not go far in telling us what exactly "moderate" means, and why we should pay attention to marginalized members of society who are unable to unsettle the democratic consensus. From a moral point of view, it will not do to say that we should only settle for compromise when some sector of society is powerful enough to resist a political decision, for morality does not stem from power.

Another reply, extremely popular among contemporary political theorists, is to emphasize the importance of the ways in which political opinions, and hence decisions, are formed in the first place. The focus is on the political process, and more specifically political *deliberation*, which covers more or less the complete process of democratic opinion formation. For advocates of this kind of "deliberative democracy" the key question is: what conditions ensure that political deliberation facilitates, or even guarantees political and moral legitimacy? This leads naturally to an emphasis on free and informed political discussion, the idea being that such discussion will lead to increased mutual understanding and reciprocal respect. Critics of the "deliberative turn" in democratic theory do not argue that discussion is unimportant. They do question, however, whether it will automatically lead to the right or best decisions and they wonder just how optimistic we are entitled to be about citizens' willingness to compromise and understand each other. Furthermore, we still need to decide whether, and how, democratic decisions should be limited by individual rights, and if so which rights. Nor can we be sure that discussion will settle this issue in the best way. In a sense, deliberative democracy presupposes, rather than shows, a certain political framework, and also a distinct set of political values.

Democratic procedures: direct or representative?

A distinction is normally made between *direct* and *representative* democracy. The former is the most basic form of democracy: you take a given issue and everyone participates in the vote. The overwhelming majority of political decisions are made through representative democracy. Here, rather than deciding on a case-to-case basis, we vote for political candidates who act as our representatives, and who are mandated to act and decide on our behalf. Much ink has been spilled on the issue of direct democracy. Some believe that direct democracy has a role to play at certain political levels (e.g. municipality-level decision-making) or with regard to some important national questions (e.g. whether a nation should join an international body such as the EU), but it is generally conceded that it cannot be the standard model of democracy in modern societies – for several reasons.

This is not to say that direct democracy would not be technically feasible. Feasibility is not the issue. Imagine you have the right to participate directly in any political decision being made in your community. Also suppose that, in general, we want people to have at least some knowledge of the issues they are to decide upon. But now imagine the time and effort you would need to devote to keeping up to date with the details of decisions on infrastructure, fiscal policies, macro-economics, and so on. Of course, the same goes for the rest of the population. In short, a massive waste of energy is involved, as compared with a system of representation in which we allow political experts and political parties to decide for us. Furthermore, the exhaustion caused by the workload of direct democracy would in all probability soon cause people to abstain from voting on anything other than their particular pet causes, and this will mean in turn that the representativeness of direct democracy would be diluted and uneven.

A further complication, pointed out by the English political theorist Adam Swift, is this. Plainly we have to vote about *something*. But who sets the agenda? We cannot vote about what we should vote on. That would result in a never-ending regress. *Someone* has to decide. But deciding what should be put to vote is often as crucial as the result of the vote. At some point we shall have to rely on representatives: they can decide which issues are put to vote. However, the difference between direct and representative democracy is now much less clear. Finally, one clear problem with direct democracy, and a possible advantage of representative democracy, is that people are not normally motivated to vote against their own immediate interests: they are often enthusiastic about voting for proposals that are advantageous to them, but reluctant to vote for proposals that mean they themselves must foot the bill. This is not *invariably* the case, of course. More often than is commonly supposed people act altruistically. Nevertheless, unless we assume that people will quite radically change their behaviour, from self-interested to altruistic, the point stands. Given this, direct democracy would seem to be a bad procedure to apply to decisions on such matters as reasonable, balanced budgets.

Pluralism, democracy and culture

In several ways, pluralism sharpens and complicates the issues. With a reasonably uniform and socially cohesive electorate, the likelihood that democratic decisions will consistently discriminate against minorities is relatively small. One does not want to make decisions from which neighbours and friends will suffer. Under pluralism, we have less in common with each other, and the risk that dominant groups will out-vote minorities on crucial matters is greater. The solution to this problem has always been to restrict the scope of democracy by granting equal and uniform rights to citizens in w a way that makes the worst excesses of "majoritarianism" impossible. However, recent developments both in politics and political philosophy have raised questions about whether this is an adequate response. A three-stage model of the struggle for rights for minorities, or the disenfranchised, helps to convey this development.

The *first battle* was fought in the name of political equality proper. It was the fight for the democratic right to vote by women, non-whites, those without property, and others. Here, the focus was on giving the *same* rights to all. Political recognition encompassed the idea that, even though we are very different in respect to sex, race, wealth, and abilities, all citizens should have the formal opportunity to participate equally in the political arena. This battle is largely over in western democracies, since no western countries today have laws that openly discriminate or disenfranchise people on the grounds of sex, race, and so on.

In the *second battle*, the picture was and is very different. Borrowing terms from the previous chapter, one might tentatively say that the first battle secured minorities a sort of *formal* political equality with the dominant group: one man or woman, one vote. However, this formal equality is entirely consistent with vast *effective* inequalities. That the law gives minorities the formal right to be represented does not mean that they are effectively represented, politically and economically. Under conditions of pluralism, we all insist on our equal *status*, but some groups are systematically underscoring in their political and economic power. This has given impetus to stronger forms of minority protection and affirmative action programs. In the first wave the fight was for the same rights. In the second it was for *different* rights for different people, but still in the name of equality.

The *third battle*, which is more recent in origin, is the most radical and controversial. Here it is claimed that even if we have formal and some sort of effective political and economic equality, under pluralism there is no guarantee of *cultural* equality. Different groups have different statuses attached to them. Thus, it is claimed, special rights or privileges or exemptions are needed to counter inequalities that are independent of, or at least different from, political and economic hierarchies. For example, in the western world homosexuals appear to enjoy economic security, but they are still socially and culturally marginalized. An issue of particular importance here concerns various national, religious and ethnic minorities. Since, or insofar, majorities in nation-states enjoys a purely contingent "cultural advantage" (e.g. the laws and the media uses the majority language; holidays and customs are defined by the majority; etc.) so-called *multiculturalists* insists that there is at least a *prima facie* reason, on grounds of equality, to compensate, or at least offer special protection to, minorities, in the form of certain "cultural rights".

There are many questions involved here. One is just how "plural" societies can be. Do we, for instance, really need the *same laws* to apply to all people, or should we rather differentiate, so that people abide by the laws of their religious affiliation in certain matters (e.g. family law)? Or, to maintain civil cohesion and solidarity, do we need to restrict some culturally distinctive practices, such as arranged marriages?

Another set of questions concerns what people owe each other. Thus it might be enquired whether people living in a democracy have a positive right – a right implying positive duties of assistance from others – to maintain their own culture. If so, what counts as a culture? Many of these questions relate directly to the discussion of choices and circumstances. To what extent should things like cultural and religious affiliation be considered matters of choice? To what extent are they circumstances beyond the individual's control?

The stance you take on these issues will affect your view of the democratic system, and especially your position on the proper scope of democratic decisions. Even more importantly, your views on what rights we have, and whether they are negative or positive, have a tremendously important influence on your attitude to pluralism – at any rate, they ought to have, if you want your views to be consistent. For instance, you might believe that people should have the right to pursue the cultural lifestyle and association of their choice. But you might not believe that people should be compensated for the eventual costs of their choices. If you see cultural and social phenomena as matters largely of choice, you will be critical of the third development mentioned above, and at least moderately sceptical about the second. Again, you will be sceptical, in general, about the legitimacy of laws grounded in considerations of culture, majority or minority.

On the other hand, if you believe that people have strong positive rights of assistance in pursuit of their cultural preferences (e.g. because you believe that culture is a circumstance), you will probably be led to endorse the third development – at least, if you also believe in political equality. You will believe that policies that protect or further vulnerable minority cultures can be legitimately grounded in culture. You might be sceptical, however, about policies that are grounded in majority culture views. Or you might believe that it is important to maintain the majority culture on grounds of its intrinsic superiority, or its ability to sustain social cohesion, or to produce equality in the long run. Given this, you will be in favour of culturally grounded policies, but only insofar as they protect and further the majority culture. As always, the picture is complicated.

Globalization and democracy

The final issue here concerns the scope of democracy in another sense: *who* should be allowed to exercise democratic influence over *which* decisions? A reasonable suggestion is that people should have the right to a say when it comes to at least the most important political issues – that is, issues that seriously affect their well-being, or rights, or interests. Whereas some issues, actions or decisions with a profound effect on us are surely not fit for democratic vote – would you agree that things such as romantic affection should be subject to democratic vote and distributed accordingly? – it seems plausible to say that all genuinely *political* decisions that will affect individuals to a significant degree ought to be under democratic control, given a plausible framework of strong rights protecting all against democratic tyranny.

If you believe people should have a democratic say in key political decisions affecting them, consider the following. We live in an increasingly globalized world. International trade, financial policies, and levels of supply and demand in the marketplace affect your chances of taking up your preferred trade and the revenue you can expect from whatever job you end up with. All the most serious environmental challenges – global warming, deforestation, and so on – are global. More and more countries are bound by international regulations and laws, by institutions like the EU and the UN, and by various treaties and contracts. Information and cultural products now flow pretty freely on the internet. In short, we are all deeply affected by decisions that are global, not local, in nature.

By contrast, democratic decisions are in almost every respect bound by *national* borders. Citizens in democratic nations vote for representatives who can, or should, represent their electorate in the relevant international institutions, but it would be absurd to claim that the global issues listed above are in general under democratic control. Many global issues have no corresponding global institution in which political representatives can exert influence, and where there are institutions, they are not democratically controlled. We might all agree that it would be best to limit global pollution. Even so, one nation might – democratically? – decide to pursue their narrow national interest and continue to pollute. And that will contribute negatively to global pollution and give the country an edge in international economic competition, as it is generally costly to reduce levels of pollution, at least in the short run.

The schism between the individual's right to exercise democratic influence over important political decisions and the manifest lack of powerful global institutions in which this democratic influence can be realized is perhaps the most pressing challenge for contemporary democratic theory, and in all likelihood it will continue to be so for generations to come. If pluralism poses a problem for democracies at the national level, it should come as no surprise that it poses an even greater challenge globally.

Key points

- The key issue raised by democracy concerns the conditions of *legitimacy* for democratic decisions.

- This becomes ever more important as societies, or polities, become more plural – in other words, as more and more evolved states include members that hold very different and incompatible views and values.

- The "scope" of democratic decisions is important when we are trying to assess the desirability of particular democratic systems or conceptions. Conceptions of democracy range from the anarchist, at one end of a spectrum, to unlimited democracy, at the other end. Anarchists believe *no* decision could even be democratically legitimate and thus limit the scope of democracy to nothing. Unlimited democrats believe that *all* decisions can be democratically legitimate and thus do not limit the scope of democracy at all.

- Direct and representative democracy should be distinguished. Direct democracy is in one sense more democratic than representative democracy, but it is vulnerable to forceful objections. Most philosophers and political theorists accept some form of representative democracy.

- The question of democracy becomes even more complicated if we include issues such as multiculturalism, minority rights, immigration and culture in general. For it could be argued that democratic systems are unjustifiably biased towards majority culture members and their conceptions of the good, values, preoccupations, and so on.

- Finally, we live in an increasingly globalized world. Decisions made, democratically or otherwise, in one part of the world seriously affect people in other parts. But if the ideal of democracy is based in part on the idea that people should have a measure of control over important aspects of their life, it seems that they should also have *democratic* influence over such decisions – even on global issues, they should have a say. This issue, of "global democracy", is probably the single most important theme in the contemporary debate on democracy.

References

Swift, Adam (2006): *Political Philosophy: a Beginners Guide for Students and Politicians*. Cambridge UK: Polity Press.

Further reading

Caney, Simon (2005): *Justice Beyond Borders: A Global Political Theory*. Oxford: Oxford University Press.

Held, David (2006): *Models of Democracy*. Cambridge UK: Polity Press. [First published 1987]

Macedo, Stephen (ed.) (1999): *Deliberative Politics: Essays on Democracy and Disagreement*. New York: Oxford University Press.

Pitkin, Hannah (1967): *The Concept of Representation*. Berkeley CA: University of California Press.

Lightning Source UK Ltd.
Milton Keynes UK
UKOW06f1800260216

269197UK00003B/174/P